# ESCAPE ROOM

## LOGIC PUZZLES

**Francis Heaney & Scott Weiss**

PUZZLE
WRIGHT
PRESS

New York

*This book is dedicated to*
Lorinne Lampert, my favorite collaborator (by Francis)

*and to*
Em, my partner in puzzling (by Scott)

PUZZLE
WRIGHT
PRESS
New York

An Imprint of Sterling Publishing Co., Inc.

ISBN 978-1-4549-4123-1

For information about custom editions, special sales, and premium purchases,
please contact specialsales@unionsquareandco.com.

Manufactured in Malaysia

2   4   6   8   10   9   7   5   3   1

unionsquareandco.com

Cover design by Igor Satanovsky
Cover images: bogdandimages/Shutterstock.com (photos),
venimo/Shutterstock.com (keyhole graphic)

# Contents

# Introduction

I love puzzles that immerse you in a story, puzzles that require you to improvise and look at things a new way, puzzles that don't follow the assumptions of what a puzzle is expected to be. Don't get me wrong, I also appreciate just solving regular crosswords, but there's nothing like the satisfaction of a puzzle that takes you on a ride through its own reality.

For a long time, before I discovered the wider puzzle community, adventure games like *Zork* or *Myst* were my primary way of accessing that sort of experience, along with the multi-puzzle extravaganzas that *Games* magazine would sometimes publish. Then I discovered in-person events like the MIT Mystery Hunt, a weekend-long puzzle marathon that, at its best, mixes storytelling, innovative puzzle construction, collaborative solving, and massive sleep deprivation into a truly one-of-a-kind experience.

But because so many of the things I enjoy in life are what some would describe as "niche," I am sometimes taken by surprise when I realize that something I think of as "a weird puzzle thing that only weird puzzle people like me enjoy" is actually quite popular. Like *Myst*! That game sold, like, a bazillion copies! (I use the term "bazillion" to avoid having to research the actual number.) Escape rooms turned out to be another example of that.

Here's the thing, though: I'm always happy to be surprised this way! I'm no fan of gatekeeping; I am honestly quite psyched for as many people as possible to enjoy the things I enjoy. And escape rooms are exactly my kind of thing. You're immersed in a story right away; the puzzles come from unexpected places; it offers a lot of "aha" moments and mini-triumphs along the way . . . and also you're done in an hour, which is honestly nice. Not every puzzle event needs to take three days.

What I hoped to do in this book was combine two things I love: logic puzzles and escape rooms. The classic "Bob owns a helicopter and never washes his laundry on Wednesday" type of logic puzzle is fun, but I don't find it very interesting to solve a lot of them in a row unless there's some kind of storyline or ultimate goal keeping me engaged. I also like a lot of variety—different puzzle formats, different themes. And one thing escape rooms do really well is offer a strong theme with a lot of variety. It seemed like the two things might work together well in book form.

I've seen a lot of escape room books that promise to recreate the full experience of a real escape room. I'm going to be contrary and say that I'm not sure a book can do that; part of what makes an escape room special is actually being in the environment. It's a theatrical event of sorts. And while I enjoy reading plays, it's not the same as going to the theater. So instead, what I've tried to do is something I think books *can* do: tell a story about the pleasures of escape rooms, through the eyes of enthusiasts.

You'll be spending time with a group of escape room–loving friends, sometimes solving puzzles about them or about the escape room they're in, and sometimes solving alongside them, trying to figure out the same puzzles they're working on (with the option of listening in on their ideas). If you'd like to have a more escape-room-y experience, we've included a section in the back of the book where you can look up combinations and passwords to see if they work or not, without having to flip to the answer section and risk spoiling yourself.

Because I wanted to season the book with as much escape room flavor as possible, I invited my longtime friend Scott Weiss to collaborate with me on it. For one thing, he's great at brainstorming on the fly, and for another, he's an experienced escape room constructor, having created several virtual escape rooms (many in collaboration with his son Em), some of which he's hosted on *Escape This Podcast*.

The hybrid format we settled on means that, although this is predominantly a logic puzzle book, it also includes a lot of escape room–style puzzles that are not strictly logic-based. There are word puzzles, environmental puzzles, and more. Since so many styles are included, we don't expect everyone to be equally good at all of them, so we've included hints to some puzzles to help get you started (particularly in puzzles where the solver is asked to figure out the instructions), and also to help simulate the process of collaborative solving.

I hope this book delivers lots of "aha" moments for you, and conveys at least a little of the immersive solving thrill that I'm trying to share. Enjoy!

—Francis Heaney

# Things to Know

Since this book has some unusual features, we've summarized them here.

**Combinations and Passwords:** If you would like to check a lock's combination or a password, consult the Combinations & Passwords section on pages 92–93. The list is organized in alphabetical order, with numbers first. The "Evolving Doors" chapter has its own section, since checking answers in that chapter requires checking two things: the combination, and the correct door. Alphabetization ignores spacing and punctuation, so, for instance, 1234 precedes 12-36-21. If your answer is not in the list at all, then of course it is not correct; otherwise, a short note after the answer will tell you if it is correct or not. If the answer is correct, it will also tell you what you find when the lock is opened.

**References:** Since the use of phones is generally not allowed in escape rooms, if a puzzle relies on trivia or other facts that players may or may not know, a reference that includes the relevant information may be placed in the room. Some puzzles here will direct you to a reference in the back of the book, but in general, if you think using your own references would be helpful, you should feel free to do so.

**Hints:** Sometimes the characters will brainstorm with each other and propose ideas. When a hint is available, a parenthetical will direct you to the page it's on. Some hints are just slight nudges in the right direction, while some may be more helpful, like full explanations of puzzle instructions (which will be indicated as such).

Special thanks to Wei-Hwa Huang, Andy Latto, Cally Perry, and Brendan Emmett Quigley for puzzle testing and suggestions.

# Flipping Out

Eleven friends (Ahmad, Bette, Ciara, Dagmar, Ewan, Frieda, Greg, Heath, Ichiko, Juan, and Kamala) were planning an excursion to one of two escape room venues in a nearby town: either Are You Ready to Lock? or Shut and Open Case. They decided to leave their decision to chance: they would each flip a coin, and if more people's coins came up heads, they'd go to Are You Ready to Lock?; if more came up tails, they'd go to Shut and Open Case. Can you figure out who flipped what, and where they decided to go?

| | heads | tails |
|---|---|---|
| Ahmad | | |
| Bette | | |
| Ciara | | |
| Dagmar | | |
| Ewan | | |
| Frieda | | |
| Greg | | |
| Heath | | |
| Ichiko | | |
| Juan | | |
| Kamala | | |

1. Either Ahmad, Dagmar, and Ewan's coin flips were all identical, or Greg, Ichiko, and Kamala's were.
2. Bette, Frieda, and Kamala's flips included two heads and one tails.
3. If only the coin flips of people whose names have more than one syllable had been counted (that is, everyone except Bette, Greg, Heath, and Juan), the final decision would have been different.
4. No two people whose names have final letters that are adjacent alphabetically (e.g., Ahmad and Bette, since D and E are alphabetically adjacent) had identical coin flips.
5. Ciara and Dagmar's flips were the same.

# Road Trip!

The eleven of them took three cars to the escape room. Can you determine who drove, who rode with whom, and where they sat?

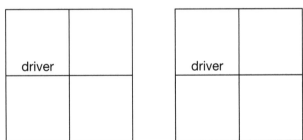

1. All the front passenger seats were occupied, and no two people seated in the front of any car had names that shared any letters in common.
2. Everyone in one of the back seats had a name that alphabetically followed the person seated in front of them.
3. No one was in a car with anyone whose initial immediately preceded or followed their own initial in the alphabet.
4. No one was seated in the same position as anyone whose name was the same length as theirs.
5. Greg doesn't know how to drive.

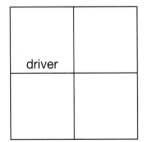

# Cabin Fever

The group chose to try out Cabin Fever, a camping-themed escape room. They were ushered into a rustic cabin and, soon after the door closed behind them, heard a thunderclap and a loud THUNK. Over the loudspeaker came an announcement: "Apologies, campers, but a lightning strike has caused a large tree trunk to fall and block the door of your cabin. No worries, though, there should be an emergency manual next to the door to help you out." Ichiko, nearest the door, plucked a brochure from a small wooden box; it read "If a Tree Trunk Has Fallen and Blocked the Door of Your Cabin." She opened it and read, "In this surprisingly common situation, simply use the emergency exit, which can be accessed with the use of four keys conveniently located within the cabin. First, ...." Unfortunately the rest of the brochure was ripped away ("Probably by a bear!," the loudspeaker interjected), leaving them to figure out how to locate the keys themselves.

# Distance Learning

At one window of the cabin, a globe sat on a table, and visible through the window was a signpost (seen at right) indicating what appeared to be distances to several cities. Ewan spun the globe and heard what sounded like a key rattling around inside it. Then he noticed that the countries lit up when he pressed on them. "Interesting," he said. After studying the signpost briefly, he turned the globe to a particular country. Can you figure out which one? (For a hint from Ewan, see page 94.)

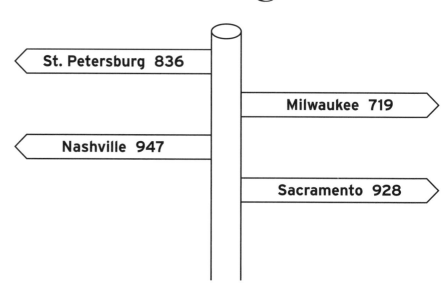

St. Petersburg 836

Milwaukee 719

Nashville 947

Sacramento 928

# Spark of Inspiration

On the mantel of the fireplace were several matchboxes resting on a box with a four-digit combination; nearby was an arrangement of matchsticks. A handwritten note taped to the box read, "Move three matches to make the two sides equal." "Should we ... just try 8418 as the combination?," Greg asked. "I expect there's a little more to it," Frieda said. Can you solve the puzzle and come up with the combination?

# Wildlife

Two other windows in the cabin (one on the north wall and one on the east) looked out on a landscape filled with forest life: birds, raccoons, and squirrels. Near one of the windows was a box with a combination lock numbered from 0 to 39; on the lid, from left to right, were pairs of silhouettes: bird + squirrel, squirrel + raccoon, and bird + raccoon. "Seems clear we need to count the animals, and that'll give us the combination," said Ciara to a group of five others (including Dagmar, Frieda, Heath, Juan, and Kamala). "Let's split up and each take one window and one type of animal—three people at each window, each counting a different animal." Can you figure out who counted how many of what kind of animal at which window, and what the final totals were (and, of course, the combination)?

1. Frieda and Juan counted different types of animals.

2. Dagmar and Kamala were at different windows.

3. No two people counted the same number of animals.

4. Twice as many raccoons were visible in the north window as were visible in the east window.

5. Ciara and Heath counted the same kind of animal.

6. Kamala counted birds.

7. Ciara counted an odd number of animals, and the amount she counted was neither the largest nor the smallest number of animals counted at her window.

8. More animals overall were visible through the east window than the north window.

9. Dagmar didn't count raccoons.

10. Kamala's count was equal to the total of two other people's counts.

11. Three people counted a prime number of animals; Dagmar was not one of them.

12. Of the people counting animals in the east window (none of whom was Frieda), one counted three less and eight less than the other two.

13. Everyone counted at least three animals; Juan counted the fewest.

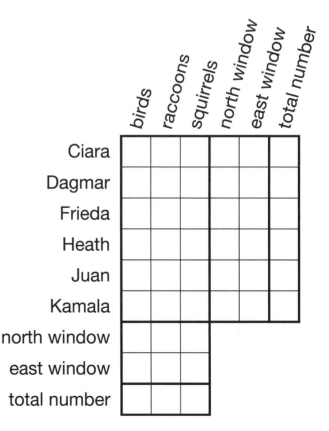

# Park It

Ahmad noticed a guest book open to a page with a writing prompt: "What National Parks Have You Visited?" Underneath was written a list of what looked like nonsense words, with question marks interspersed. "This is obviously a cryptogram," said Ahmad. From a nearby bookshelf, Bette called, "Hey, I found a brochure with a list of every National Park—do you need it?" "Nah," Ahmad replied, "I think I got this." "Okay," Bette said, "but it was sitting on this box with a four-digit lock, so maybe they're related." (If *you* would like to see the list in the brochure, you can find it on page 94.)

---

## What National Parks Have You Visited?

UNWWZAFO???

UZFNIT?N

DEONAEU EPX?

SZFKLE O??N

XPEO?P WEQN

XEYTOZW PNN?

DWEX?NP

JNEOK ?EWWNU

IEIIZOK XEG?

QNRET ?SZPJF

K?O FYPTRDF

JPU OZPO?DEF

NGN?DWEJNF

---

# Under Log and Key

After finding all four keys (a red one, a blue one, a silver one, and a gold one), the group faced another problem: there were no obvious keyholes anywhere. But then Ewan was looking at a framed photo on the wall of the Loch Ness Monster and remarked, "Hey, that's weird, there's a lamp in the background of this photo that looks just like the one on that table over there." Ichiko slapped her forehead, saying, "Loch ... lock ... someone pick up that lamp." The lamp, attached to the table by a hinge, was quite heavy, but sure enough, underneath it was an inconspicuous red keyhole, in which the red key fit. Three other pictures of Loch Ness led them to a record player, a statue, and an umbrella stand. Four of the friends lifted the heavy items out of the way while four others turned their keys in the revealed keyholes simultaneously. There was then a loud "click" from the fireplace, and the three remaining friends tugged on the mantel, revealing that the fireplace concealed a hidden door, which they all sauntered through with time to spare. Can you determine what each friend was doing in this climactic moment?

1. No two people who sat in the same seat on the drive to the escape room (in the puzzle on page 7) had the same role—that is, holding a key, lifting an object, or moving the fireplace. No two people who sat in the same car were a pair at the same keyhole.

2. No one who stood at the east window counting wildlife (in the puzzle on page 9) was standing at the fireplace, and none of those three were paired up with each other.

3. Juan had tweaked his back at the gym, so he was unable to lift any heavy objects.

4. The three people at the fireplace had names of different lengths.

5. The silver key was held by one of the women (that is, Bette, Ciara, Dagmar, Frieda, Ichiko, or Kamala), and the statue was lifted by one of the men (that is, Ahmad, Ewan, Greg, Heath, or Juan). These two items were not a pair.

6. Ahmad wasn't holding a key.

7. Greg and Kamala were paired up at one of the keyhole locations, but not the gold keyhole.

8. Both the person with the red key and the person they were paired with had been seated in the back of a car.

9. The blue keyhole was not beneath the umbrella stand.

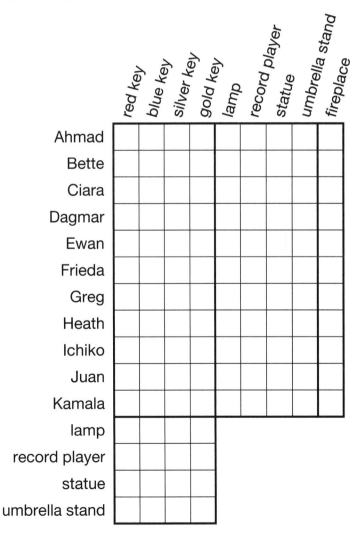

# Don't Get Booked

After completing Cabin Fever, most of the group needed to head home, but Ahmad, Dagmar, Ewan, and Ichiko stuck around to do one of the venue's other escape rooms, Don't Get Booked. In this scenario, the solvers were playing a team of rare book thieves who had broken into a library after hours to infiltrate the rare book room. Unfortunately, the room was equipped with an advanced defense system, locking itself as soon as the team entered, while also sending an alert to the police (who, the team was informed, would arrive in exactly one hour). This changed the goal from the planned heist to simply "getting away without being arrested."

# Bio Engineering

Adjacent to a small wall safe with an alphabetical keypad was a rolling book cart that had a shelf filled with biographies, arranged as shown below. On the side of the cart was a label that read "TO BE ALPHABETIZED." "That's strange," Dagmar remarked, "Agamemnon, Alighieri, Calloway, Hammerstein ... looks to me like they're already *in* alphabetical order. There must be something we're missing." Ewan leaned in and asked, "What about these symbols on the bottom of the spines? Looks like Morse code." Ichiko piped up from across the room, "Well, there's a Morse code key right here if you need it." (If you need it too, you can find it on page 94.) She tossed it across the room. After a moment, Ewan frowned. "Nope," he said, "That's just gibberish." Can you figure out what to do next, and what to type on the keypad to open the wall safe?

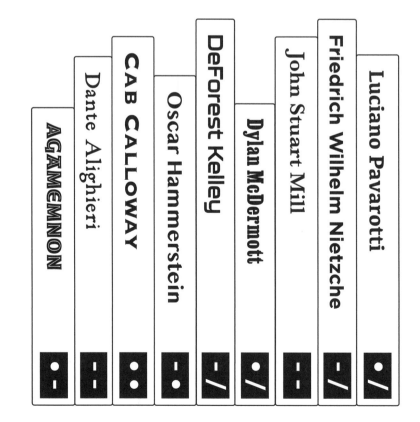

# Playing Tags

After opening the wall safe and finding the book inside, Ahmad said, "There's actually tons of books all around the room. What makes this one different?" "I dunno," said Ewan, "Maybe we'll use some of these other books too. Anyway, take a look at this!" On a desk was a note that read, "Hey, fellow librarians! I wrote an 8×8 sudoku in your honor! It has all your names in it, reading horizontally or vertically, always from left to right or from top to bottom. There's also a little something extra in there (just a recommendation if you're in the mood for something escapist)." The sudoku itself was on a separate piece of paper, surrounded by the nametags of the other librarians. Can you complete the sudoku and find the "something extra"?

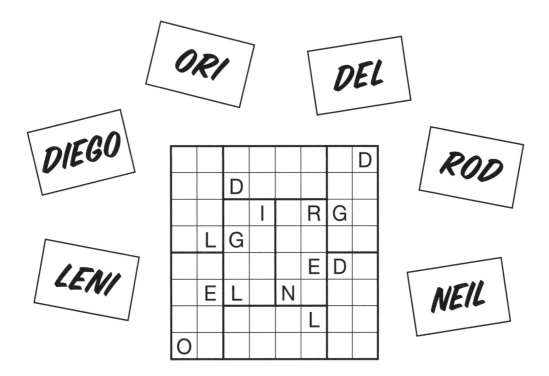

# Little Blank Books

Ichiko noticed a library poster on the wall (seen at right) and noted, "Looks like one of those promotions that encourages people to read more." Dagmar replied, "I think it actually *does* inspire me to pick up a book." She then scanned the books around the room and grabbed one. Which book?

## Find Your Next Book!

| | |
|---|---|
| AUGUSTA | RANGE |
| HEARD | TIMERS |
| LANED | WALL |
| PLAY | WART |
| PLIGHT | WART |

*The* ___ *of the* ___ by Richard Ford

*The* ___ *of* ___ by Sun Tzu

___ ___ by Charles Dickens

___ *in* ___ by William Faulkner

___ *My* ___ by Sabaa Tahir

# Dewey or Don't We?

One of the prominent items in the room was a locked box with a 5-digit combination lock and a round red sticker on the lid. That red sticker matched one on a list marked "Books Needing Classification" that listed the following book titles:

- *F=ma: The Most Important Equation*
- *How to Avoid Self-Incrimination in Court*
- *Playing the Hot Corner*
- *Recipes for your Independence Day Celebration*
- *The Battle of the Somme*

The group was stymied until someone noticed the Dewey Decimal System subject chart on the wall, seen at right. With the use of that poster and a little help from an encyclopedia in the room (you may similarly allow yourself a little online research if needed), they soon figured out the combination to the lock. Can you?

001–099: Generalities (encyclopedias, reference books, odd occurrences)
100–199: Philosophy and Psychology
200–299: Religion and Mythology
300–399: Sociology and Law
400–499: Languages
500–599: Mathematics, Physics, Chemistry, and Biology
600–699: Applied Science (inventions, transportation, cookbooks)
700–799: Arts, Recreation, and Sports
800–899: Literature
900–999: Geography and History

# Shelf-Help Group

Having found four hidden books throughout the room, the group discovered a schematic inside a desk drawer detailing the way to disable the room's defense system and unlock the door: The four books must each be placed in the center of one of the 16 shelves lining the walls of the room (four identical sets of four on each wall) while standing on a specific step of the four-step ladder in front of each bank of shelves. Can you figure out which shelf each book needed to be placed on, who placed each book, and which ladder step each was standing on? (Note that you will need the titles of the four books found around the room to solve this puzzle; this information can be found in the answers to the individual puzzles, or summarized on page 94.)

1. Exactly one book needed to be placed along each wall, with no two books placed on shelves at the same height. Similarly, each person stood on a different rung of their ladder.

2. The step of each ladder required to unlock the door never corresponded to the shelf upon which the book on the same wall was to be placed. (For instance, if the book on the north wall needed to be placed on the bottom shelf, then the required step of the ladder on the north wall was not the bottom step of the ladder.)

3. The book on the highest shelf was one whose title becomes two new words if its initial letters are replaced by the initial letters of one of the other books. (That other book was on the east wall.)

4. It's possible to switch the positions of two books so that the titles would be either alphabetized from top to bottom or from bottom to top.

5. The people standing on the two lowest ladder positions were directly across from each other in the room. The books on the two lowest shelves were not directly across from each other.

6. Ahmad stood on the top step of his ladder but found it very awkward to place his book from there, since he needed to reach all the way down to the bottom shelf.

7. Dagmar stood on the north ladder.

8. The book on the west wall had a title whose two words were the same length.

9. Ewan stood on a higher rung than Ichiko.

10. The two books whose titles have the same number of letters as each other were to be shelved on adjacent walls.

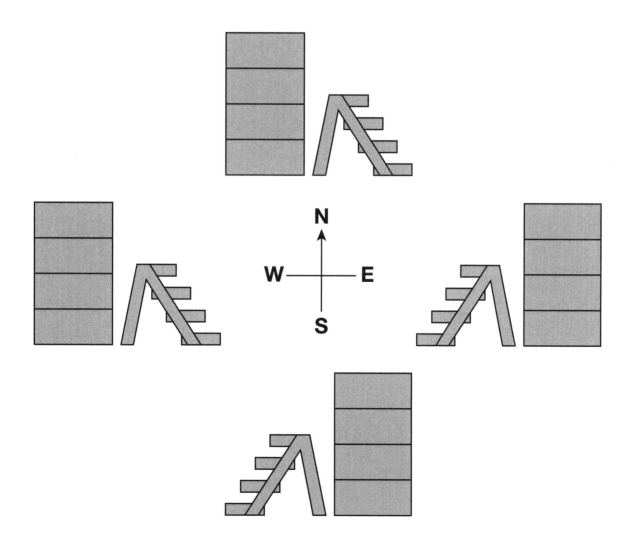

# Saturday Sundaes

The next Saturday, Kamala returned with four other friends (Lily, Malik, Nelson, and Olga) to do the library escape room she'd missed. Before that, however, the five stopped at a nearby ice cream parlor for sundaes, each getting two different scoops of ice cream and two different toppings, choosing from the menu seen at right. Can you figure out what everyone ordered?

1. No two people ordered the same combination of ice cream flavors; similarly, no two people ordered the same combination of toppings. Every ice cream and topping was ordered at least once.

2. One person's order consisted entirely of flavors and toppings in which the words were in alphabetical order, and another's order consisted entirely of flavors and toppings in which the words were *not* in alphabetical order.

3. All of Malik's toppings and ingredients had a word in their names that shared an initial.

4. One of the toppings was only chosen by Olga.

5. Neither of the two people who chose vanilla coriander ice cream topped their sundae with diced almonds.

6. Nelson did not order peppermint watermelon.

7. The only person who ordered cinnamon maple ice cream (who was not Olga) also ordered diced almonds.

8. Kamala and Lily's sundaes had at least an ice cream flavor in common, while Kamala and Nelson's sundaes had at least a topping in common.

9. One person ordered peppermint watermelon ice cream with hot fudge; all four items ordered by that person were each ordered by exactly one other person.

10. At least two people ordered butterscotch chips.

11. Lily and Malik's sundaes had no ingredients in common at all.

---

**Menu**

*ice cream flavors:*
**vanilla coriander
chocolate habanero
strawberry rhubarb
cinnamon maple
peppermint watermelon**

*toppings:*
**hot fudge
crushed pineapple
butterscotch chips
diced almonds
whipped cream**

---

| | vanilla coriander | chocolate habanero | strawberry rhubarb | cinnamon maple | peppermint watermelon | hot fudge | crushed pineapple | butterscotch chips | diced almonds | whipped cream |
|---|---|---|---|---|---|---|---|---|---|---|
| Kamala | | | | | | | | | | |
| Lily | | | | | | | | | | |
| Malik | | | | | | | | | | |
| Nelson | | | | | | | | | | |
| Olga | | | | | | | | | | |

# Cosplay and Crossbones

The group breezed through the library room and decided to continue on into a pirate-themed room called Cosplay and Crossbones, in which the premise was: you are the captain and crew of a small private yacht that has been captured by a pirate ship. However, these are not the most hard-bitten buccaneers out there. In fact, they're a group of pirate movie superfans who were inspired to give the piratical arts a try after watching *Treasure Island* one too many times. They've thrown you into the brig and told you that if you're able to escape before they tow your ship to shore, you're free to go. If you fail, you'll be forced to watch a full marathon of every *Pirates of the Caribbean* movie (with a discussion period after each one), so the stakes are high.

# Oh, Grate

As the door locked behind them, the friends noticed the brig was nearly empty: not a puzzle in sight. Apart from the stone walls, there was only a ramshackle cot with a single pillow on it and a grate in the wall near the floor. Kamala lay on the cot for a moment to think and felt a lump in the pillow. "Hey," she said, "There's a screwdriver in here!" She quickly brought it over to the grate only to find that it only fit one of the eight screws, most of which were nonstandard, with slots in the shape of different multi-pointed stars, as shown here (in their correct arrangement, although not to scale). Everyone quickly started searching the rest of the room, finding more screwdrivers in the mattress, under floorboards, behind loose rocks in the wall, and so on. In short order they'd unscrewed the grate to reveal a crawlspace which led to ...

well, before we get to that, can you first figure out who found which screwdrivers, and in what order they went through the crawlspace?

1. The slots of the screws, starting in the upper left and going clockwise around the edge of the grate, were shapes with 2 points, 3 points, 5 points, 7 points, 11 points, 13 points, 17 points, and 19 points.

2. Everyone found either one or two screwdrivers, and gave themselves a score for each screwdriver corresponding to its number of points. The person with the highest total score went through the crawlspace first, and the rest followed in descending order. No two people had the same score.

3. Malik scored five points less than Nelson.

4. Three people had scores that were consecutive numbers; Lily, who only found one screwdriver, had the middle score of the three.

5. Kamala found screwdrivers that unscrewed two corner screws.

# X Marks the Spot

The group emerged from the crawlspace into what appeared to be the captain's quarters, with maps on the walls, a pair of bunk beds, and various pirate paraphernalia scattered around. On one table was a small chest inscribed "X Marks the Spot," with a five-letter lock; the chest was decorated with an island map upon which a 5×5 grid was superimposed, as shown at right. Nelson said, "Upper berth packs lotsa words, eh?" He lifted himself up to the top bunk, which held a heavy book labeled "Captain's Log," and which contained five similar-looking maps, numbered 1 to 5, tucked among the pages. The text of the captain's log is below, and the five maps appear on the next page.

---

**Jan. 5**
Heard on the RADIO that the Coast Guard was near. The FATES were on our side, and we were able to make a quick U-TURN to ELUDE them.

**Jan. 29**
For MOVIE night we RERAN the OPERA adaptation "The Pirates of Penzance." It HASN'T aged well; the plot TWIST is pretty contrived. Audience got ANTSY.

**Feb. 17**
NOLAN is hosting a VITAL meeting to ENACT new bylaws and said he'd send "an EVITE with the DEETS." I reminded him to speak more pirate-y, and pointed out his LASER gun was also inappropriate.

**Feb. 21**
Practicing calligraphy (my ESSES need work) as we approach Greece. Planning to visit the AGORA to buy AGAVE, SUMAC, and some ITEMS for our cheese TRAYS.

**Mar. 14**
New pirate just joined: ELISA from IDAHO, a former Senate aide for Ben SASSE. Seems ambitious; she better not try to USURP me.

**Mar. 25**
When the hours LATEN and time FLITS by, I love feeling the ship LURCH as the WAVES SLOSH against the hull. Sometimes I fire a cannon just to enjoy the ECHO'S reverberation.

**Apr. 18**
Arrived in Tanzania; "JAMBO, DEARY," the friendly dockmaster called to us, and we JAWED with him for a bit. BRETT wanted to see OASES but I told him the desert wasn't nearby. Tomorrow we set off for PAPUA New Guinea.

---

May 5
The sun SHONE mercilessly on our weekly poker game. "My UVEAS are burning," said AUDRA, squinting, as she ANTED.

May 12
ADELA has been reading about the SYNOD of bishops, and she's obsessed. She got a tattoo of a SPIRE, decorated her room with photos of church ATRIA, and I just saw her TRY ON one of those cardinal hats.

May 26
SILTY coffee today. Must PLEAD for more filters, and perhaps DOWSE for fresher water.

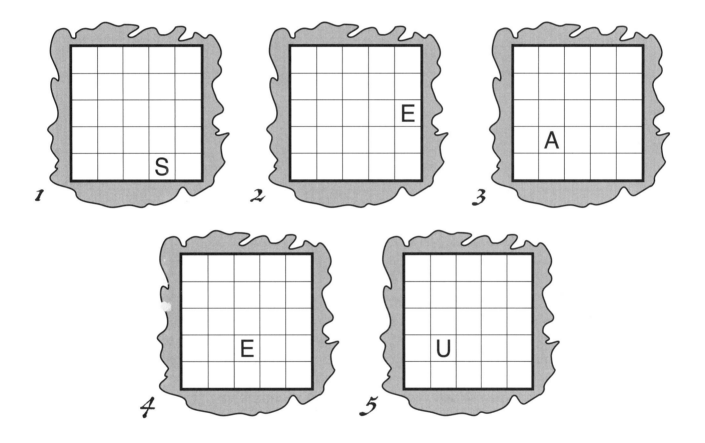

"That is indeed a lot of words," Nelson said. Lily peered over his shoulder; "I see what to do with this," she said, explaining her idea to the rest of the group. (If you'd like Lily to explain it to you too, see page 94.) The five of them each took a map and set about filling them in, which didn't take them long. But then they were stymied for a bit until Malik had an insight, retrieved the chest, did some cross-referencing, and spun the wheels of the lock to spell a five-letter word, which opened the chest. Can you figure out the combination? (If you'd like to hear Malik's insight, see page 94.)

# X Marks the Spot Again

"Pirates really do love treasure chests, I guess," Olga remarked, plucking another chest off a shelf and hoisting it in the air. It had the same "X Marks the Spot" inscription, as well as an eight-letter alphabetic lock and, she saw after examining it more closely, a small plaque inscribed as seen at right. Kamala looked at the plaque and said, "Ah, I think that goes with this piece of parchment I saw on the desk." Upon that piece of parchment was the puzzle grid shown here.

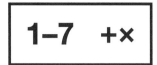

"There must be instructions somewhere," Malik said, "Let's spread out and look." "No need," Lily interrupted, "I know how this type of puzzle works. It's a calcu-doku variant." Nelson leaned in, saying, "Oh, so it's a Ke—" "No, Nelson, it's actually not the same thing, if you'd let me finish," Lily continued, "The numbers on the plaque mean this puzzle uses the digits 1 through 7. Each row and column will contain every digit from 1 to 7 exactly once each. Each region with a dark outline is called a cage, and each cage has a numerical clue in the upper left corner. Now, normally there's a mathematical symbol after each clue. For instance, a 15+ clue means that the digits in the cage add up to 15, while a 15× clue means that the product of all the digits in the cage is 15. Numbers are allowed to repeat within a cage as long as they obey the rule that no two identical digits are in the same row or the same column. Now, what's different about this calcu-doku is that the mathematical symbols are missing from the grid, so we have to logically figure out which symbol goes with each clue. The two symbols on the plaque mean that we're only using those two symbols."

Working together, they filled in the grid, and thanks to one insight from Malik, followed by another from Olga, they cracked the eight-letter combination. (If you'd like to find out what either of those insights were, turn to page 94, where both are listed separately.)

# X's Continue to Mark Spots

Kamala stood in front of a very large map. "This is a very large map," she said, accurately. It was in a wooden frame and had ten X's on it, which were labeled with the numbers 0–9 from north to south. The X's were raised, and pressing one caused the corresponding number to appear on a nearby 10-digit display. "Looks like this frame is on hinges," said Olga, "There must be something behind it. We just have to press the X's in the right order ... whatever that is." "Here's a notebook labeled 'Safely Retrieving All Ten Treasures'," said Malik, "Let's see what it advises."

1. The X's represent treasures, which you must collect in a specific order. The dotted lines represent safe paths between the treasures. Well, "safe" may be overstating it; they can only be used once, as each will collapse behind you as you walk on it, thanks to some very implausibly advanced technology made out of natural materials. Each treasure may also only be visited once, except by ghosts, whom you will see plenty of.

2. Three of the treasures have paths that lead to coves, in one of which you will have time to stash a rowboat before landing. (These locations are marked on the map with sailboats, because I draw better sailboats than rowboats.) You may use that boat once and only once to travel to one of the other coves to continue collecting treasures.

3. The route may start from any treasure, even one that isn't near the shore. (What, you don't think we have a hang glider?) Same thing goes for the last treasure; at that point, just run for it, there will probably be like five boulders rolling toward you.

4. A swarm of bees lives near the fourth treasure; you'll want to head straight for a rowboat after retrieving it. From there, it will still be possible to choose either cove to get your next treasure, but it will be impossible to visit all ten treasures if you pick the wrong one.

5. There's a path between the third treasure and the last treasure.

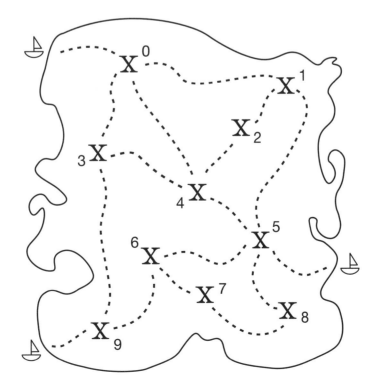

# Polly Gone

Continuing to examine items around the room, the group marveled at a shelf containing a collection of busts of famous one-named musicians: Beck, Beyoncé, Bono, Brandy, Cher, D'Angelo, Des'ree, Drake, Hozier, Liberace, Madonna, Pharrell, Prince, and Usher. "Strange choice of decor," Olga remarked, "Maybe this is the playlist for their ... *pirate radio station*." Everyone acknowledged that they saw what she had done there. They also discovered a note on the desk that read, "Don't forget to feed Polly." "That must be a parrot," Nelson said, "and there is a birdcage over there. But it's empty." "Mm, well, look at this other note," Kamala said. She handed over a second piece of paper that read, "Don't forget to lock the birdcage." Nelson nodded, saying, "I guess we need to find the parrot. But where do we start?" Lily called from across the room, "Have you looked at the papers on the bottom of the birdcage? They're pretty interesting. These shapes kinda look like busts." The various bits of paper can be seen below and at the top of the next page. After completing the puzzle, the group had an idea where the parrot ought to be, but it took some searching to find it. Can you figure out what they needed to look for?

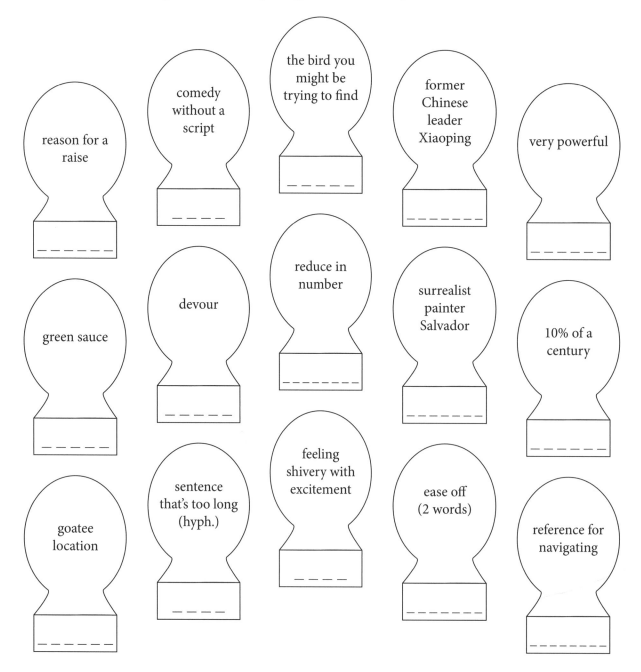

### Left

- Conservative's opposite (7)
- *Encanto* character that they don't talk about (5)
- Swing back and forth on a string, say (6)
- Mast or boom, on a pirate ship (4)
- Medicine-making biz (6)
- Monthlong celebration in June (5)
- Namesake of an NFL video game (6)
- Place of residence (4)
- Taking advantage of (5)
- They hang from curtain rods (6)
- Traveling by yacht, say (7)
- Tree limb (6)
- Type of ape, for short (5)
- Tyrannical ruler (6)
- Word after "great" or before "Meat" (6)

### Right

- Common name for a dog (5)
- Decomposing (7)
- Elvis's Mississippi birthplace (6)
- Jay of late night TV (4)
- Magazine that's "Where Black Women Come First" (7)
- Main course (6)
- More like a posh hotel (7)
- Name that rhymes with "Leicester" (6)
- Puff from a joint (4)
- *Raiders of the Lost Ark* hero, for short (4)
- Rhythm for parade marchers (7)
- Second word in the title of the song used for Rickrolling (5)
- Shampoo in a green bottle (5)
- What a collar circles (4)
- Wonderland visitor (5)

For a hint on how to get started, see page 94. For full instructions to the puzzle (except for the final step), see page 95. You can also find a hint about the final step on page 95.

# The Well-Dressed Pirate

Once they had retrieved Polly the parrot from its hiding place, Malik noticed something in a photo on the desk. "Hey, that parrot is in this photo of the captain, on his shoulder. And the captain's wearing all the other things we've found! I think maybe the way to get out of the room is to dress up like the captain and just … ask one of the pirates to let us out?" "Worth a try," Lily said, donning all the accoutrements and pounding on the door. A little peephole opened and an eyepatch appeared, followed by a grunt of annoyance as the pirate swapped to the other eye. "Ah! Captain!," he said, "Locked yourself in again, did ye? Well, just tell me the passphrase so I know it's you and I'll let ye right out!" "Oh, ah," Olga said, "The passphrase?" "Yes, you remember, to protect against impersonators. Well, if you forgot the passphrase again too, I think ye wrote a note to remind yourself. Now if you'll excuse me, I have plunder to inventory." And with that, he shut the peephole. They returned to the desk and found a nondescript envelope they had overlooked, which they opened to reveal the instructions on the next page.

# Passphrase Reminder

1. Write down the eight-letter phrase that was the answer to the calcu-doku puzzle.

   _____

2. Reverse that, then, at the end, add the five-letter combination to the puzzle with the 5×5 squares.

   _____

3. Find the name of a famous bear, and add the musician from the missing bust before its last letter.

   _____

4. X marks the spot; change the letter X to the Roman numeral equivalent of the three-digit number you get when you take the 3rd, 4th, and 5th digits from the combination to the map puzzle in the wooden frame.

   _____

5. Find a sequence of three alphabetically consecutive letters and swap the positions of the first two.

   _____

6. Find a doubled letter and change both letters to the last vowel that appears in the string.

   _____

7. Move the thirteenth letter to the end.

   _____

8. Move the twelfth letter to the beginning.

   _____

9. Add a W somewhere in the string to make a synonym for "memorized."

   _____

10. Delete the first and last letter of the synonym you just spelled.

    _____

11. Find a chemical element and delete everything but its first letter.

    _____

12. Delete every G and H.

    _____

13. Find a farm animal, and replace its last letter with the title given to a knight.

    _____

14. Reverse the first three letters and delete the middle letter of the three.

    _____

15. Take the eleventh and twelfth letters and place them around the center letter.

    _____

16. You should now have the passphrase (as well as a description of what's kept you locked up).

# The Queen's Game Bits

After escaping the pirate-themed room, the group was joined by Ichiko and Juan (who had just finished taking a yoga class nearby) and together they all started a new room, The Queen's Game Bits. First, the escape room staff ensured that everyone in the group was familiar with the rules of chess and chess problems (as you ought to be before attempting most of the puzzles in this section), and then they were informed that they were all members of a college chess team who had signed up for a personal "From Rookie to Queenie" coaching session with Bobby Fischer's second cousin once removed, Queenie Fischer. Turns out that "eccentric recluse" genes must run in the family, because when the group was ushered in for their coaching session, she was nowhere to be seen; all they heard after the door clicked behind them was her voice over a loudspeaker saying, "The best training I can give you is to teach you how to think under pressure. I've locked you in my chamber of chess memorabilia and left you some clues about how to escape. If you do not escape after an hour ... I mean, I'll let you out, obviously, but I'll be very disappointed in you. Good luck! No refunds!!"

# Going Overboard

"I feel like there's too many pieces on this board," said Ichiko, looking at a chessboard sitting next to a suitcase with a 4-digit numerical lock. "There are definitely a few extraneous ones," Nelson said. "But I see what to do." Can you figure out the combination?

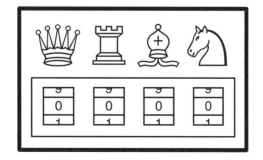

# Break It Up, Matey

Resting on a side table with a single drawer, locked with an eight-letter alphabetic lock, was the array of items seen below, plus a short note reading, "This board has been broken up into eight 2×4 pieces (without rotating any pieces). After the board has been correctly reconstructed, White is to move and mate in 1. You will also notice that some squares have numbers painted on them. Those do not affect chess play, but may be useful later." "Okay," Kamala said, "Now if I remember the rules of chess problems correctly, which I hope I do since I was asked about that specific thing before we came into this room, White is always moving up the board, and Black is moving down." "Yes, among other things," replied Juan. (To hear more of Juan's recap about chess problems, see page 95.) "Wait," Malik said, "There are three black knights! Is this even a legal board?" "Black must have promoted a pawn," Juan said patiently, "Perfectly normal. Now let's give this a try." The group proceeded to work together, experimenting with various arrangements until they found the only legal board position for which White had a mate in 1; you may find it useful to make a photocopy of this page so you can cut out and rearrange the pieces yourself. "Now let's see what the password is," Lily said. (If you want a hint from Lily about how to find the password, see page 95.)

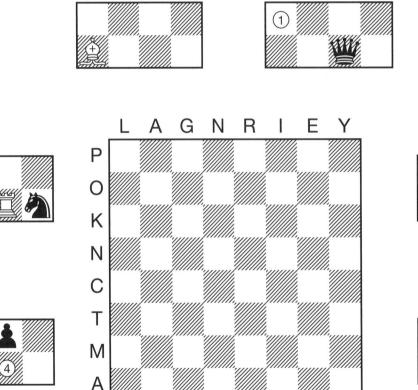

# Knight Game

"Oh, this is a novelty," said Olga, plucking a piece of paper taped to a wall safe, "A puzzle with instructions. Thank goodness Juan showed up. Juan, you're the sudoku expert, this one's for you." Juan took the paper and perused it. "Let's see ... 'This is an anti-knight sudoku. It follows all standard sudoku rules, but in addition, no two identical digits may be a knight's move apart.' Oh, yeah, this is exactly my jam." "That's good," Nelson said, looking over his shoulder, "Because we've only got an hour and this looks like it would take me all day." (If you find yourself feeling the same way as Nelson and would like an easier version of the puzzle, see page 95 to add two more givens.) The sudoku and the wall safe's lock are shown below. Can you solve the sudoku and find the combination?

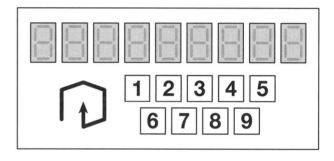

# I Was Told There'd Be No Algebra

While Juan was busy with the sudoku, Kamala called everyone else over to look at a notepad, tucked in the side pocket of a suitcase locked with an 8-letter alphabetic lock. "It's a pad for tracking the moves of a chess game," she said, "It's got the first 8 moves of a game written down in algebraic notation." Malik leaned in, nodding sagely and saying, "Right, right ... but remind me what that is?" Kamala said, "It's simple; from White's perspective, the rows of the board are labeled 'a' through 'h' from bottom to top, and the columns are labeled 1 to 8 from left to right. But what I was about to say is, the game doesn't look right. The first move is legal, but none of the others are. And this is written on the page underneath. Here's what I think ..." The relevant parts of the pages are shown here. Can you figure out what's going on and find the combination? (If you want to hear what Kamala thinks, see page 95.)

| Qa4-a6 | Re1-a3 |
|--------|--------|
| Na3-e8 | Ba4-h7 |
| Pe1-h7 | Ke8-h2 |
| Na5-g2 | Ba5-e6 |

- Backs of necks
- Clean up in the tub
- Eddie who founded an outdoor gear company
- Fictional creature whose "hide" is used as a leather substitute
- Fuzzy fruit, in French
- Host country of 2022's World Cup
- Plot summary of a TV episode
- Singer who once used a dollar sign in her name

# Weighted Pieces

Along one wall a set of shelves were filled with seven scales (five balanced, two unbalanced), on which chess pieces had been attached. A whiteboard on the side of the shelves displayed a chart of 12 chess pieces, as well as 12 numbered magnets that fit into blanks next to the pieces. "Seems safe to assume each type of piece weighs a different amount from 1 to 12," Ichiko said. "And that we'll need the information to open this safe," added Malik, indicating a combination lock above which this was inscribed:
[♙+♟+♘+♞] − [♗+♝+♖+♜] − [♕+♛+♔+♚].
Can you find the weights of all twelve pieces and determine the combination? (Note that an unbalanced scale only indicates which side is heavier, and nothing else about the relative weights.)

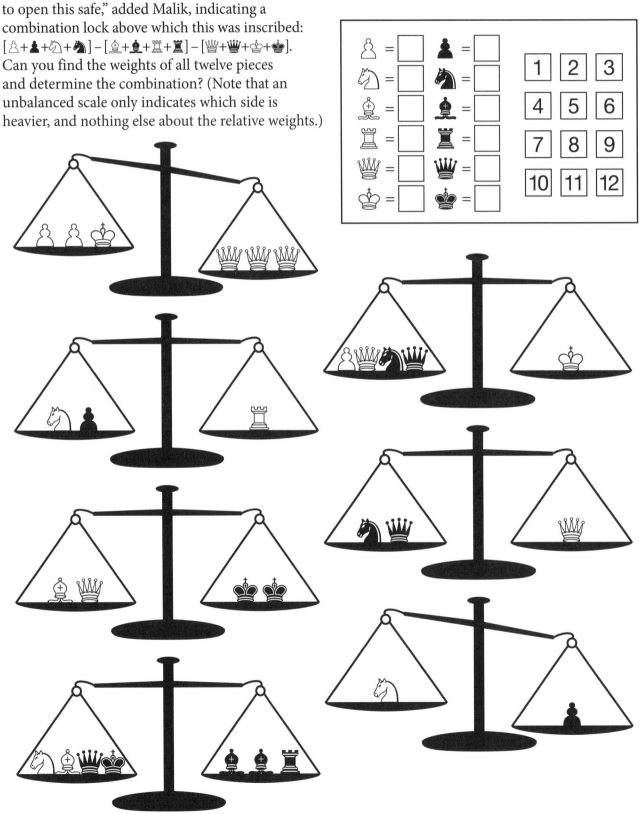

28

# Words of Wisdom

Kamala checked her watch and said, "Uh-oh, we haven't got much time left ... how's that sudoku going, Juan?" "Almost done," he called from the other side of the room, "Feel free to come help!" "We'd just slow you down," Olga said, "Besides, we've got another puzzle to get through." A copy of *Chess Life* magazine was open to an article written by Queenie Fischer herself. The photo accompanying the article showed Queenie's hands typing on the keyboard of an old IBM desktop computer—the same one that was on a table nearby, blinking with a prompt for a seven-letter password. The article read as follows:

---

*Greetings, readers. I've gained enlightenment from a lot of chess greats over the years: Michael ADAMS, Viswanathan ANAND, Levon ARONIAN, Fabiano CARUANA, Max EUWE, Bobby FISCHER, Anatoly KARPOV, Bent LARSEN, Emanuel LASKER, Vera MENCHIK, Ruy LOPEZ, Judit POLGAR, Alexei SHIROV, Nigel SHORT, Boris SPASSKY, and Wilhelm STEINITZ, to name just a few. They've taught me strategy, centeredness, and the importance of getting lots of rest. If you study the passage below, you might learn from them as well, by seeing what they've picked up along the way.*

Once, a chess champion lost her room's pass key and couldn't get in. She had muffins—cherry ones—inside, and she was starving. Her last tournament had gone poorly (she'd fasted in it): zero wins. She checked the gift shop for food: LOL ... Pez dispensers, but no Pez. She was hungry enough to eat a tadpole garnished with algae. Soon she would fall like Icarus, an arrogant failure. But then someone handed her a flask serenely.

"I could see you were unwell," her savior Horatio said. The flask contained a banana daiquiri. It gave her the energy to go buy macaroni pancakes.

She returned, planning to set her alarm sensibly early. "Thanks, Horatio," she said. He replied, "No need to tell me I'm a mensch; I know. I always keep a flask in my shirt, over my heart. It's because my kinfolk are poverty-stricken. Now go win that tournament like the stellar damsel you are!"

*I thought calling me a damsel was slightly condescending, but nonetheless, I was very grateful. Yes, that's right, that chess champion was me! Did I go on to win that tournament? No, I slept right through my alarm and missed the whole thing. Oversleeping is the only thing I'm better at than chess. Anyway, hopefully you learned something.*

---

"I guess I did learn something," Lily said after making many notes on the sheet, "but what I ended up with is way longer than seven letters." (If you're stumped and would like instructions for how Lily got to this point, see page 95.) "I think we just need to interpret it correctly," Nelson said, "What if we ..." He trailed off and started making his own notes on top of Lily's, and between them, they soon found the password. (If you'd like hear the rest of what Nelson was about to say, turn to page 95.)

# Knights of the Round Table

Just as Lily and Nelson had finished with Queenie's computer, Juan let out a cry of triumph as he finally opened the safe. With the retrieval of the last of the twelve hidden knights (which were, as a reminder, white, silver, pink, red, orange, yellow, green, blue, purple, gold, gray, and black), there was a music sting and a dramatic lighting change: a spotlight focused on a square table in the middle of the room, whose corners suddenly fell to the floor, leaving a perfectly round table. Additionally, twelve indentations had appeared around the table, evenly spaced, one marked with a star. "Quickly!," said the booming voice of Queenie, "You must return the knights to their rightful places around the table! Only then will you be able to leave the room! Well, either that or when the hour runs out. Good luck!" And with that, the speaker went silent. Olga quickly placed all twelve knights around the table randomly; nothing happened. "Well, it was worth a shot," she said, "Anybody see anything helpful?" Malik found a book entitled *Seating Etiquette for Medieval Party Hosts*, which gave them all the information they needed to place the knights and make their exit. See if you can figure out each knight's name, nickname, age, and position at the table.

1. The twelve knights were Sir Agravain, Sir Bryan, Sir Clarence, Sir Dinas, Sir Edward, Sir Fergus, Sir Geraint, Sir Hector, Sir Ironside, Sir Jerome, Sir Kay, and Sir Lionel. Each had a nickname that corresponded to the color of one of the knights (the White Knight, the Silver Knight, and so on).

2. The knights must be seated clockwise in order from eldest to youngest, with the eldest knight seated in the position marked with a star.

3. The youngest knight was older than 20, and the oldest knight was younger than 90. No pairs of knights who sat next to each other had the same difference in ages.

4. The Blue Knight, who was not Sir Dinas, sat directly opposite Sir Clarence.

5. Sir Edward was five years older than the Gold Knight.

6. Sir Bryan, Sir Lionel, the White Knight, and the Purple Knight were seated in four adjacent seats, not necessarily in that order.

7. The Pink Knight, Sir Hector, and the knight who was 42 years old were spaced evenly around the table.

8. Sir Kay's age was the sum of the ages of the Orange Knight and Sir Fergus.

| | the White Knight | the Silver Knight | the Pink Knight | the Red Knight | the Orange Knight | the Yellow Knight | the Green Knight | the Blue Knight | the Purple Knight | the Gold Knight | the Gray Knight | the Black Knight |
|---|---|---|---|---|---|---|---|---|---|---|---|---|
| Sir Agravain | | | | | | | | | | | | |
| Sir Bryan | | | | | | | | | | | | |
| Sir Clarence | | | | | | | | | | | | |
| Sir Dinas | | | | | | | | | | | | |
| Sir Edward | | | | | | | | | | | | |
| Sir Fergus | | | | | | | | | | | | |
| Sir Geraint | | | | | | | | | | | | |
| Sir Hector | | | | | | | | | | | | |
| Sir Ironside | | | | | | | | | | | | |
| Sir Jerome | | | | | | | | | | | | |
| Sir Kay | | | | | | | | | | | | |
| Sir Lionel | | | | | | | | | | | | |

9. Sir Dinas and the Purple Knight were seated an equal distance from the eldest knight.

10. The colors in the nicknames of the two knights seated on either side of Sir Ironside were complementary (i.e., red and green, blue and orange, or yellow and purple). Another pair of complementary-colored knights sat next to each other.

11. The Yellow Knight was twice the age of the Black Knight, who was twice the age of the Red Knight.

12. The Green Knight's age difference with one of his neighbors was twice his age difference with his other neighbor; this was also true for both the Pink Knight and the Silver Knight. The only three knights not involved in those three sets of relationships were Sir Ironside, the Gray Knight, and the Orange Knight (two of whom were the oldest and youngest knights).

13. Two people sat between Sir Agrivaine and the Gray Knight.

14. Sir Lionel was not the Silver Knight.

15. Sir Geraint was older than Sir Jerome.

16. The Black Knight was seated within three seats of the Pink Knight.

17. Sir Dinas was 9 years older than the knight seated to his left.

18. More of the knights' ages were evenly divisible by 7 than by 5.

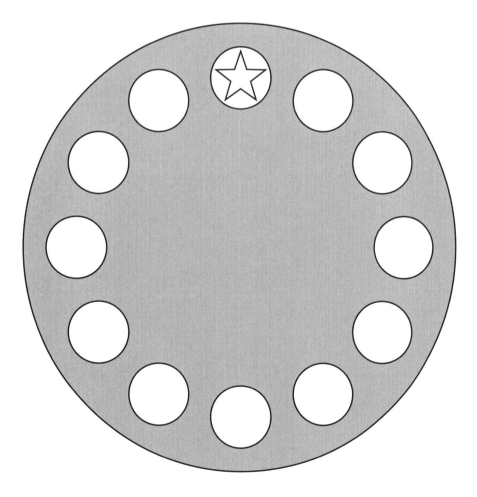

# Escape Plans

The following Saturday was a particularly busy one. Only ten of the friends were available (Ahmad, Bette, Ciara, Dagmar, Ewan, Frieda, Greg, Heath, Ichiko, and Juan), and all of them were busy at various times throughout the day. They soon realized it was impossible to get their schedules to coincide, and they decided that they would pick the time slot for which the most people were available. Can you figure out at which times everyone was available, who went to the escape room (and which one), and when?

1. The choice this weekend was between two escape room destinations: Come In and Get Out (which offered one-hour appointments starting at noon with the last appointment at 6:00) and The Great Escapes (which offered one-hour appointments starting at 12:30 p.m. with the last appointment at 6:30).

2. Bette and Frieda were both invited to a birthday party and had to be done by 4:30 at the latest.

3. Everyone whose name started with a vowel was available for exactly 90 minutes, and no two of them were ever available at the same time.

4. Greg was available for three 90-minute blocks, but he was busy with other things for at least 60 minutes between each of those blocks. He and Ewan were never available at the same time.

5. Neither Ahmad nor Heath could start until 3:30 at the earliest.

6. The one person who had the shortest uninterrupted time slot of availability (one single half-hour, which wasn't very helpful) was also the one person who had the longest uninterrupted time slot of availability.

7. Ciara had to leave her schedule open from 2:00 until 4:00 for a FedEx delivery, but she was definitely available from 4:00 to 4:30 at least.

8. Ewan was hosting an audition and wasn't available from 1:00 to 4:00.

9. Heath and Frieda were each available for a single uninterrupted block. Heath was available for twice as long as Frieda was, and their availabilities overlapped by exactly one hour. Additionally, among the times Heath and Frieda's schedules overlapped Greg's, each had one overlap of exactly one consecutive hour (but that hour was not the same for both Heath and Frieda).

10. Juan, Ichiko, Bette, Ciara, and Dagmar, between them, had available non-overlapping time slots of five different lengths that accounted for every half hour of the day, in that order from the start of the day to the end. (Some of them may have had other available time slots, separated from the five mentioned already in this clue by at least a half hour.)

11. There were exactly two half-hour time slots in which only one person was available; they were consecutive.

12. One person had exactly three time slots available, each of which was one hour long.

13. Dagmar was available, in total, for one hour more than Juan was.

14. No time slot that Bette had was the same length as any time slot that Ciara had.

15. Six people went to the escape room. There were two other one-hour slots for which five people were available.

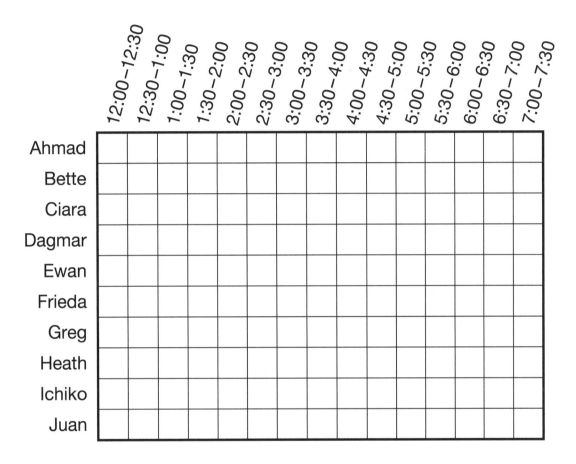

# Evolving Doors

The group of six opted to try Evolving Doors, a room with an unusual premise; it's a series of small rooms that each contain multiple doors. The doors display instructions about which door is the exit and how to open it. However, the doors have evolved to have consciousness, and now the doors don't always tell the truth.

# The First Room

As the entrance door closed and locked behind the group, they saw two doors on the opposite wall, and a plaque next to them that read:

One door always
tells the truth.
The other door
always lies.

Above the knob of each door was a numerical keypad that controlled a four-digit locking mechanism. Signs on the two doors read as follows:

### Door 1

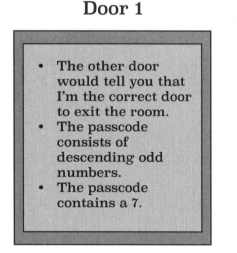

- The other door would tell you that I'm the correct door to exit the room.
- The passcode consists of descending odd numbers.
- The passcode contains a 7.

### Door 2

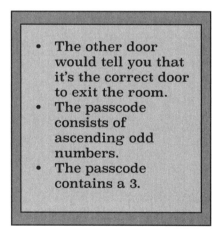

- The other door would tell you that it's the correct door to exit the room.
- The passcode consists of ascending odd numbers.
- The passcode contains a 3.

A voice over the loudspeaker said, "You are free to try to guess the passcode if you get stuck on any puzzle, but an incorrect guess will prevent you from trying again for one full minute." Clearly, it's better to be sure. So which door is the correct door, and what is the passcode?

# The Second Room

In the next room, there were three doors, with this accompanying plaque.

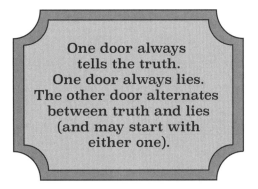

One door always
tells the truth.
One door always lies.
The other door alternates
between truth and lies
(and may start with
either one).

Above the knob of each door was an alphabetic keypad that controlled a four-letter locking mechanism. Signs on the three doors read as follows:

## Door 1

- Door 2's second statement is a lie.
- The password contains two or more of the letters in the word CHAW, in those positions.
- The correct door's third statement is a lie.

## Door 2

- Door 1's first statement is the truth.
- I am not the liar.
- The password contains two or more of the letters in the word CLAP, in those positions.

## Door 3

- Door 2's third statement is a lie.
- The password contains two or more of the letters in the word SLOW, in those positions.
- The password contains two or more of the letters in the word CHAP, in those positions.

Which door is the correct door, and what is the password?

# The Third Room

Proceeding onward, the group was faced with four doors and another plaque. The doors' locks were once again outfitted with alphabetic keypads.

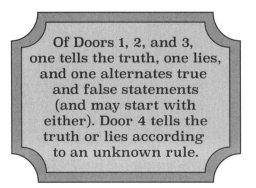

Of Doors 1, 2, and 3, one tells the truth, one lies, and one alternates true and false statements (and may start with either). Door 4 tells the truth or lies according to an unknown rule.

### Door 1

- Door 4 is telling the truth when one of its statements has an odd number of words, and lying when one has an even number.
- Either Door 3 or Door 4 is the correct door.
- The password is a country.

### Door 2

- Door 4 is telling the truth when one of its statements begins with a vowel, and lying when one begins with a consonant.
- Either Door 1 or Door 3 is the correct door.
- The password is something seen on a sports field.

### Door 3

- Door 4 is telling the truth when one of its statements does not use the letter A, and lying when one does.
- The password is a word meaning "loyal."

### Door 4

- "Retweet," for short, is in the solution.
- Use the brief version of "post office" in your set of letters.
- The word between "spare" and "expense" must appear in your final answer.
- Opposite Free Parking on a Monopoly board are these two letters of the password.
- More letters you'll need will be found in the very center of the French novelist Victor.
- One pair of letters in the password is the start or end of Bowie's Ziggy.
- The state that borders OR and ID appears in the sequence.
- Include Gore, Green, Roker, or Unser in your code.

Which door is the correct door, and what is the password?

# The Fourth Room

In the next room, the group saw something unexpected: the same number of doors as the previous room. Also a plaque. The doors featured numerical keypads.

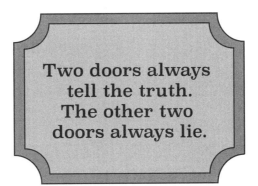

Two doors always
tell the truth.
The other two
doors always lie.

## Door 1

- If you asked Door 2, "Would Door 3 say that Door 4 was a liar?" but didn't hear the answer, Door 4 would tell you that Door 2 said "No."
- The combination is the product of two prime numbers, one of which is 47.

## Door 2

- If you asked Door 4, "Is Door 1 or Door 2 the correct door?" but didn't hear the answer, Door 1 would tell you that Door 4 said "Yes."
- The combination is the product of two prime numbers, one of which is 89.

## Door 3

- If you asked Door 1, "Is Door 1 or Door 3 the correct door?" but didn't hear the answer, Door 4 would tell you that Door 1 said "Yes."
- The combination is the product of two prime numbers, one of which is 67.

## Door 4

- If you asked Door 2, "Would Door 1 say that Door 2 or Door 3 is the correct door?," Door 2 would say "No."
- The combination is the product of two prime numbers, one of which is 71.

Which door is the correct door, and what is the combination?

# The Fifth Room

In this room, not only were there four doors with alphabetic keypads, there were four plaques:

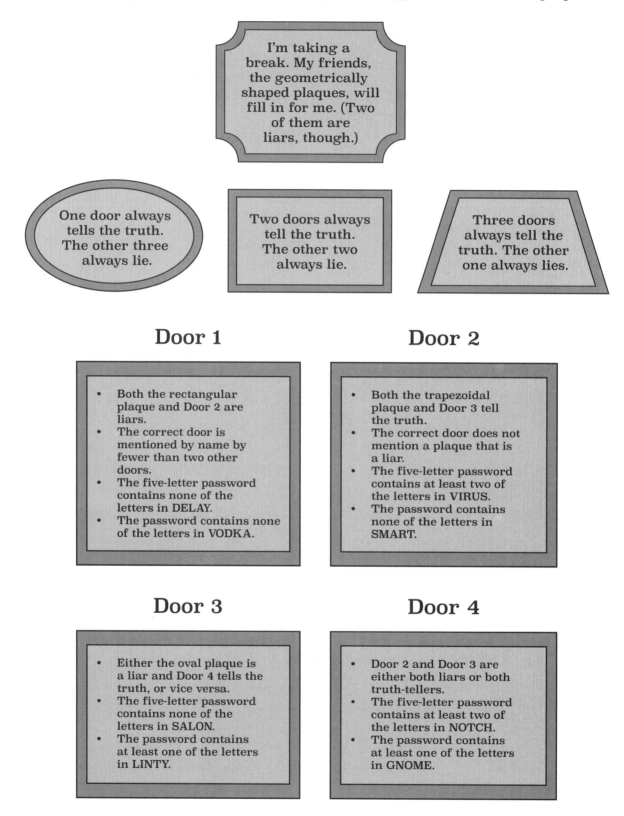

I'm taking a break. My friends, the geometrically shaped plaques, will fill in for me. (Two of them are liars, though.)

One door always tells the truth. The other three always lie.

Two doors always tell the truth. The other two always lie.

Three doors always tell the truth. The other one always lies.

## Door 1

- Both the rectangular plaque and Door 2 are liars.
- The correct door is mentioned by name by fewer than two other doors.
- The five-letter password contains none of the letters in DELAY.
- The password contains none of the letters in VODKA.

## Door 2

- Both the trapezoidal plaque and Door 3 tell the truth.
- The correct door does not mention a plaque that is a liar.
- The five-letter password contains at least two of the letters in VIRUS.
- The password contains none of the letters in SMART.

## Door 3

- Either the oval plaque is a liar and Door 4 tells the truth, or vice versa.
- The five-letter password contains none of the letters in SALON.
- The password contains at least one of the letters in LINTY.

## Door 4

- Door 2 and Door 3 are either both liars or both truth-tellers.
- The five-letter password contains at least two of the letters in NOTCH.
- The password contains at least one of the letters in GNOME.

Which door is the correct door, and what is the password?

# The Final Room

When the group got to this room, they were surprised to see that, although a plaque was on the wall as usual, there were no signs hanging up on any of the three doors; instead, they were lying on the floor, next to a bowl containing six colored keys (red, orange, yellow, green, blue, and purple). A voice came over the loudspeaker, "Oh, uh ... sorry, we've been meaning to finish this room, but no one's ever made it this far, so we kinda lost track of it. We'll give you a free voucher if you want to come back later." "Can't we just hang the signs up?," several of the group asked in unison. "I forget which sign goes where, sorry. I mean, if you want to try figuring it out, you can have some extra time. Word of warning, though! Don't assume that a sign isn't on Door 1 just because it says something about Door 1; doors can talk about themselves in the third person. Or should that be 'in the third door'? Well, anyway, good luck!" It took a lot of discussion, but the group was eventually able to figure out which sign belonged on which door, and which key to use on which door to escape. Can you do the same?

> One door always tells the truth.
> One door always lies.
> The other door alternates between truth and lies (and may start with either one).

- Door 1 is the alternator.
- The truth-teller's door is the correct door.
- The correct key is red, orange, or yellow.

- Door 2 is the liar.
- The alternator's door is correct and/or Door 3 is correct.
- The correct key is red, blue, or green.

- Door 3 is the truth-teller.
- My previous statement was true.
- The correct key is green, orange, or purple.

# Card-Carrying Puzzlers

Eight of the friends (Ahmad, Ciara, Ewan, Greg, Ichiko, Kamala, Malik, and Olga) decided that on Saturday they would visit the venue that the group hadn't visited the previous week. On Friday night, Ewan said, "I have a proposition. Let's deal a hand of poker with no drawing; everyone plays exactly what they're dealt. Whoever has the highest hand wins, and whoever has the lowest hand pays for the winner's ticket to the escape room tomorrow, whoever has the second-lowest hand pays for the person in second place, and so on," and everyone agreed. Given the following facts about the game, can you determine exactly what cards everyone held, and who paid for whom? (A reminder of the ranking of poker hands is below, if you need a refresher.)

---

**Straight flush:** Five cards in sequence, all of the same suit (e.g., ♥J ♥10 ♥9 ♥8 ♥7); the highest straight flush (A, K, Q, J, 10) is called a royal flush.

**Four of a kind:** Four cards of the same rank, plus one card of another rank, called a "kicker" (e.g., ♠K ♥K ♣K ♦K ♥2).

**Full house:** Three cards of the same rank and a pair of cards of another rank (e.g., ♠5 ♥5 ♦5 ♣A ♦A).

**Flush:** Five cards of the same suit, not all in sequence (e.g., ♣Q ♣10 ♣9 ♣6 ♣5).

**Straight:** Five cards in sequence, not all of the same suit (e.g., ♠8 ♦7 ♠6 ♣5 ♥4).

**Three of a kind:** Three cards of the same rank, plus two cards of two other ranks (e.g. ♥4 ♣4 ♦4 ♣A ♦6).

**Two pair:** Two cards of the same rank, two cards of another rank, and one card of a third rank (e.g., ♠J ♦J ♥10 ♣10 ♠3).

**One pair:** Two cards of the same rank, and three cards of three other ranks (e.g., ♥8 ♦8 ♠K ♥J ♣9).

**High card (a.k.a "nothing"):** Five cards that don't form any of the above hands (e.g., ♥A ♣J ♦8 ♣6 ♠2).

---

1. Before dealing, Ewan discarded every card in the deck lower than a 5, which meant the eight hands dealt used up every card in the deck exactly.

2. No two players held the same hand. The lowest hand was one pair, and the highest hand was a royal flush, rather impressively.

3. The player who had a straight held no red cards or face cards.

4. If (and only if) they had combined their cards, Ewan and Ichiko could have made a royal flush; of the two, Ewan's hand ranked higher.

5. Between them, Greg and Olga held all four 7's.

6. The three aces not included in the royal flush were all among the four lowest hands.

7. The flush contained only two cards of consecutive ranks.

8.  Ahmad held the ace of diamonds and the 9 of spades.

9.  Ciara held no 10's.

10. The player with four of a kind held a heart kicker.

11. Malik's hand ranked higher than Ciara's, whose hand ranked higher than Greg's, whose hand ranked higher than Olga's. The four of them each held one of the 8's.

12. Between them, the player with two pair and the player with three of a kind held three kickers of the same suit. That suit was not included in the three of a kind.

13. Kamala's hand contained at least one heart.

14. The player with the king of spades held no other card higher than a 10.

15. The pair held by the player with one pair contained no clubs.

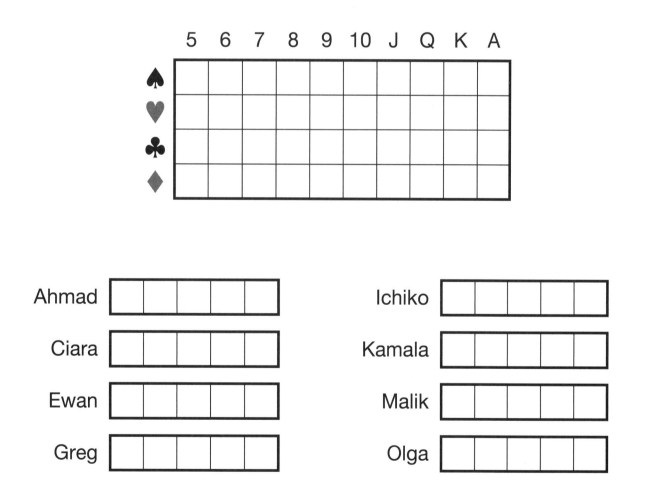

# Astray in Space

The group signed up for Astray in Space, for which they received the following introduction: "You are the crew of a spaceship whose navigation computer has massively malfunctioned, leaving you adrift with no clue as to your location. You might say you were lost, even. To leave the ship, you will have to safely land on a friendly planet, which you won't be able to find until the computer is repaired. You'll also need to repair the ship's main console, since all the instrument displays exploded when the computer malfunctioned. And you'll need to do all of that quickly, because the ship's oxygen supply will only last one more hour. The situation is quite dire, but fortunately there is a helpful robot on board that can remind you how everything works. Less fortunately, she needs to be recharged. Good luck, and may the forceps be with you. (That's the only tool that can open Rosalie's box of power cables.)"

# In a Case of Emergency

"Well, I guess the first thing to do is to find those forceps," Ichiko said, "Oh, here they are. Or at least, here's the case they are in." Immediately next to the door they had entered (beneath a large decorative diagram of our solar system) was a sturdy case reading "Emergency Forceps." The case also had the below phrases printed on it, along with an eight-digit locking mechanism:

**GNU THIEVES**

**HUNT ERASURE**

**MIXES CURRY**

**PUREE JOINT**

**RAZORS TUNE**

**RISEN MAN**

**STEER HAVEN**

**UPTOWN TEEN**

Olga said, "I see what we need to do." (If you'd like to hear Olga explain it fully, see page 95.) The group made short work of the list of phrases, and soon had an eight-digit number ... which did not work. "Oh, derp," said Greg, "I know where we went wrong." This time the case opened with no trouble, and they turned their attention to recharging the robot.

# Rosalie the Robot

Ciara picked up Rosalie's box of power cables and used the forceps to twist a tiny, deeply inset latch on the front. Opening the box revealed four cables. Rosalie's back panel had seven ports which needed to be connected by the four cables to charge her battery; the box of cables included the helpful set of instructions below.

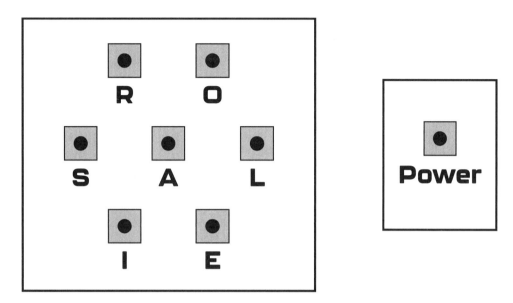

1.  Three pairs of ports must be connected to each other; the seventh must be connected to a nearby power source.

2.  Of the three pairs of ports to be connected on Rosalie's panel, at least one pair is in a direct horizontal line, and at least one pair is in a direct vertical line.

3.  Exactly one cord connects a pair of letters that both fall alphabetically between the two letters connected by another cord.

4.  No more than one cord connects two consonants or two vowels.

When they connected all the cords properly, they could hear something that sounded like a power surge, but Rosalie stayed inert. They then saw that she had a power button on her left shoulder ... which was unfortunately behind a locked panel. The panel had a small keyboard and a six-letter display. Ewan sighed, "Well, now what?" "Not to worry," Malik said, "I see what the password must be."

Can you figure out how the cords were arranged, and what password opens the panel?

# Star Search

Now that her power was restored, Rosalie's face lit up (literally) and she greeted the group. "Hello! How can I help you? I gather we're in danger." Kamala took the lead and said, "Rosalie, we need to fix the navigation system. How do we do that?" Rosalie let out a series of endearing beeps, then said, "That's simple. Just access the navigation control panel and press the big red button to reboot the system. The control panel is right behind that star chart on the wall, just behind you. It is kept locked, though." The group turned to see a large grid of letters with no stars on it whatsoever. "This is not full of stars," said Ahmad, "At least not that I can see." "Well, it's an interactive chart," Rosalie explained, "Here's something that will help you." A printout emerged from a slot in her right hand. As the group took it, she added, "Once you find the password, just type it into the keyboard below the chart." The printout and chart are shown below.

| | |
|---|---|
| A STAR IS BORN | |
| BUENOS TARDES | |
| CORNSTARCH | |
| COSTA RICANS | |
| CUSTARD PIE | |
| CUT THE MUSTARD | |
| GUEST ARTIST | |
| LONE STAR | |
| LOST ARK | |
| REST AREAS | |
| SEA STAR | |
| STAR TURN | |
| STAR WARS | |
| START MENU | |
| TELSTAR | |
| TONY STARK | |
| TRISTAR | |
| VACANT STARE | |

```
L O O S C U H D P I E
K S E D O O N E U B D
W A A I V T R H I N M
O E N T A Y E N O L U
T M I W C H E O F S M
O E S N A C I S O C E
N R B L N R U T E T H
Y A O R T S S M F O T
R I R R O T T E L U T
K H N E E S E N C R U
E T S I T S E U G T C
```

"This looks like a word search," Greg said, "But I don't see any of these words in here." Ichiko leaned over and said, "Well, what if ..." (If you want to hear the rest of what Ichiko said, turn to page 95.) After the group was finished with the list, they weren't sure what to do next, but Ewan noticed something. (If you'd like to know what that was, see page 95.) He zipped through the next step and typed a long phrase on the keyboard without thinking. When that didn't work, he took a moment to think and then typed in a shorter password, which was correct. Can you figure out the password?

# Constellation Prize

As soon as they pressed the button to reboot the system, a nearby screen lit up with six diagrams, and a list of six phrases. "Excellent!," said Rosalie, "The system is back online and ready to scan six nearby constellations for habitable planets to land on. But ... oh, no, it looks like the labels on the stars were corrupted when the system crashed, so you'll need to relabel them." "The what now?," Ciara asked. "The navigator labeled all the constellations according to mnemonics he used," Rosalie explained, "He never explained the system to me, but those were his six mnemonics for those six constellations. Anyway, the computer won't be able to chart a path through any of the systems until it knows which star is which. Well, just do your best. Once you're sure everything's correct, enter the password to activate the navigation system." "But how do we know which mnemonic goes with which constellation?," Kamala asked. Rosalie beeped supportively and replied, "I can give you hints if needed." (See page 95 for Rosalie's hints.) She went on, "But like I said, just do your best."

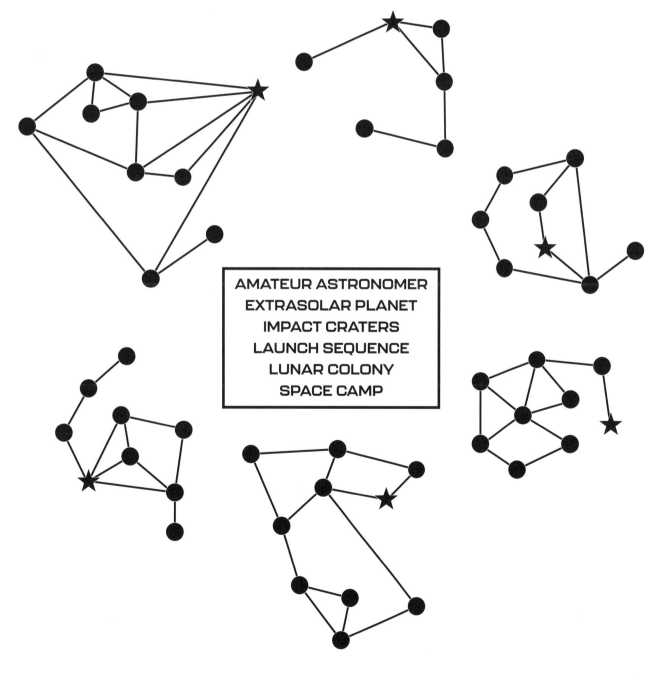

AMATEUR ASTRONOMER
EXTRASOLAR PLANET
IMPACT CRATERS
LAUNCH SEQUENCE
LUNAR COLONY
SPACE CAMP

# You Could've Fueled Me

"Good work," Rosalie said, after the group had activated the navigation system, "The ship's computer has found a suitable planet and plotted a course. We should be on our way momentarily." At that moment, a large red light on the console started blinking. "That seems bad," said Malik. "Oh, it is," Rosie replied, "Very bad. Apparently the fuel system has also gone offline, so we can't move. You'll need to reconstruct the schematics for the filtration units. Each filtration unit is a square grid in which every square contains a pipe section. The network of pipes must be laid out so that it connects the fuel lines at the upper left and lower right, and the pipes form a fully connected network. The filtration unit is supported by regularly spaced rods, indicated as circles on the schematic. A square containing numbers indicates the number of rods surrounded by any completely enclosed area that includes that square. Any square that contains parts of multiple enclosed regions contains a separate number for each one. I can show you an example." Rosalie produced another printout from her hand:

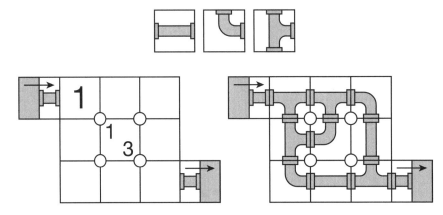

"At the top," she explained, "you'll see the only three kinds of pipe you may use, which can be rotated into any orientation. You may not use any four-way connections or pipe caps. Below that, on the left is a sample schematic, with the pipes correctly placed on the right. Some pipes may be pre-placed in the schematic; those cannot be moved or otherwise altered. There are three filtration units. Once you've reconstructed them all, just enter the password into this console, and we can be on our way." "What about these notes on the right of the schematics?," Olga asked. "I think those are part of the password reminder," Rosalie said. Can you restore the schematics and find the password?

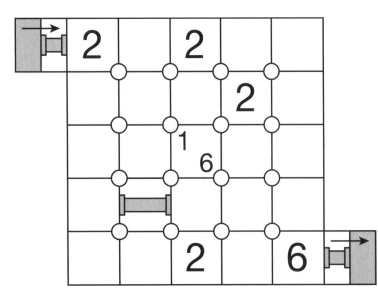

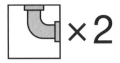

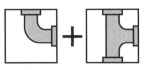

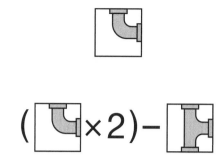

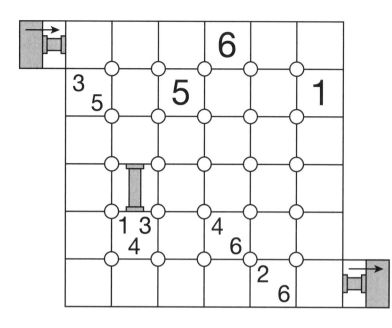

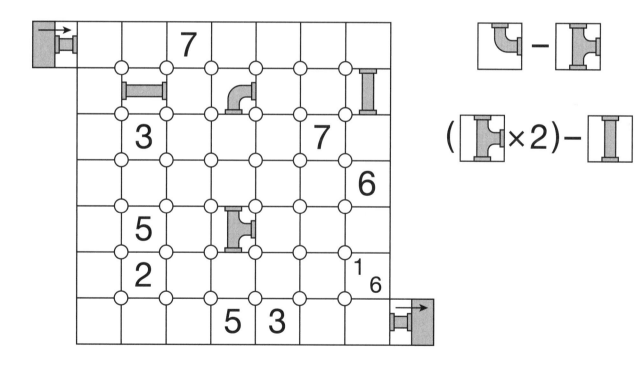

# Landing of the Lost

Rosalie let out a somewhat disappointed beep. "You guessed the password without finishing the puzzle!" "We've only got an hour here, Rosalie," Ewan said, pragmatically. "I took notes so I can solve the last grid later." "Well, I guess that's fine," said the robot, "In any case, seems like we're moving, so now we need to repair the control panel. There are seven controls: four dials and three sliders. The three sliders are working normally, but the small circular displays around the four dials are broken. You'll need to read the instructions carefully to reconstruct the landing sequence." They took the instruction printout from her hand, which read:

> Label the four dials from left to right using the passwords from Rosalie's control panel, the navigation control panel, the constellation charts, and the fuel filtration units, in that order. Start with the top circle, and enter the letters clockwise one by one. If, on any dial, you are about to enter a letter that already appears on that dial, change that repeated letter by moving it ahead 13 places in the alphabet (wrapping around from Z to A if needed). The three sliders may each be set to any letter of the alphabet, or may be individually deactivated and reactivated by flipping the switch. After every step of the landing sequence, the readout (that is, the letters that the dials are pointing to, and the letters on the activated sliders) must spell a word from left to right. After the final step of the sequence, enter that word into the computer to land the ship.

"Well, that part sounds straightforward enough," Greg said, "But where do we find the landing sequence?" "I think it's in the shredder," Rosalie said. Greg groaned. "What?? No! Why?" "I think it was for security reasons," Rosalie explained, "The pilot had it memorized, so she didn't see the need to keep it around. But you might be able to piece it back together." The group took the lid off the paper shredder, tucked away inconspicuously beneath the control panel, and found the strips of paper seen on the next page. They identified the first step easily enough, but sorting out the rest was going to take some effort. Can you piece the instructions back together and land the ship? (If you'd like to make sure your control panel is labeled properly, you can double-check it on page 96.)

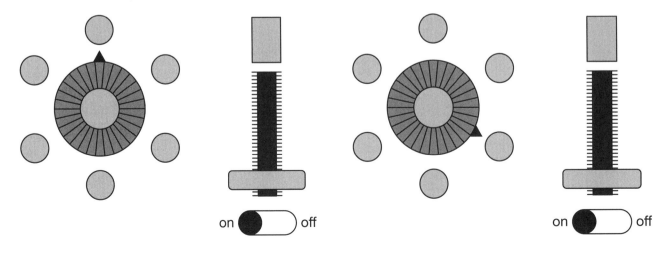

The dials are preset for the first step of the sequence, so simply set the sliders to another term for a flying saucer, except with the last letter changed to another letter you can make by erasing part of it.

Turn the third dial one letter clockwise, then set the second and third sliders so they match the first slider.

Turn the first dial two letters counterclockwise and the second dial one letter clockwise. Change the third slider to the previous letter in the alphabet.

Turn the first dial to the opposite letter and the second dial one letter counterclockwise. Deactivate the third slider and set the other two sliders to a brain measurement.

Turn the third and fourth dials two letters clockwise, deactivate the second slider, and change the third slider to the opposite compass point.

Turn the first and third dials two letters clockwise, then set the sliders to the end of Captain Picard's first name, spelled backward.

Turn the second dial two letters clockwise and the fourth dial one letter counterclockwise. Set the sliders to a word meaning "covered with frost," with the first letter moved to the end.

Turn the third dial to the opposite letter and the fourth dial one letter clockwise. Reactivate the slider that's turned off and set it so it matches the slider to its left.

Turn the first dial two letters clockwise. Reactivate the slider that's turned off and set the sliders to a six-sided solid used in games.

Turn the first dial one letter clockwise and the third dial two letters counterclockwise, then reactivate the slider that's turned off and set the sliders to the abbreviation for Connecticut, preceded by the last letter of its capital.

Turn the second dial one letter clockwise and the fourth dial one letter counterclockwise. Set the sliders to one of the stars of "Rocky III."

Turn the second dial to the opposite letter and the third dial two letters clockwise. Set the sliders to an abbreviation meaning "that is," spelled backward.

Turn the third and fourth dials to the opposite letter. Set the sliders so they spell a phrase heard at a wedding.

Turn the first and second dials one letter clockwise, then set the sliders to the French word for "sea," with the first letter moved to the end.

Turn the first dial one letter clockwise and the fourth dial two letters counterclockwise. Change the first and third sliders to the compass point that's 90 degrees counterclockwise.

Turn the first dial two letters counterclockwise and the third dial to the opposite letter. Set the sliders to the Phoenix Suns' sports league, shifted 17 letters ahead in the alphabet (wrapping around from Z to A if needed).

Turn the second dial two letters clockwise and the fourth dial to the opposite letter. Deactivate the first slider and set the other two to a college degree.

Turn the second dial to the opposite letter and the third dial one letter counterclockwise. Set the sliders to a term for a male child, except with the last letter changed to another letter you can make by erasing part of it.

Turn the first dial two letters counterclockwise, then set the sliders to the notes in a C major triad.

Turn the fourth dial to the opposite letter, then set the sliders to another name for a vinyl record, spelled backward.

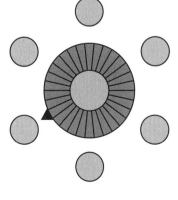
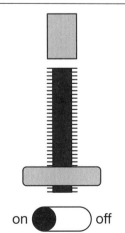
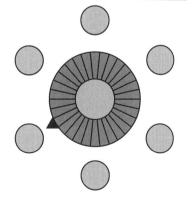

on ⬤ off

# Raiders of the Lost Arcade

Having successfully landed the ship (and purchased souvenir Rosalie pins), the group decided to push on into another room, Raiders of the Lost Arcade. The host explained, showing them into the room, that they were a group of vintage video game connoisseurs investigating a hot tip about an original Pong machine in mint condition, rumored to be locked in the back room of Robot Genie's Cybercastle, an abandoned arcade on a deserted section of the Jersey Shore boardwalk. They've only got one hour before a rival group of collectors will swoop in and claim it like they ALWAYS do, with the locksmiths and lawyers they keep on retainer. Can you get the best of them this time?

## Basket Case

"Oh, *heck* yes!!," said Ciara, heading straight to Basket Case, one of those skill games where you sink baskets to win prize tickets. "I'm great at this game! I can sink so many baskets in 30 seconds, you won't believe it. Oh, wait, I guess it's not a speed game this time. The sign says 'Throw five perfect shots to win.' Well, that's easy." She easily sank five baskets in a row ... and nothing happened. "I guess we've got to do something else," Kamala said, "What's this writing on the ball?" "Oho," Ciara replied, "Interesting." Ciara studied the text, thought about it for a moment, then threw the basketball five more times, after which bells rang and the machine spat out a chain of prize tickets. Can you figure out exactly what she did? (You can check the five steps individually in the password checker.)

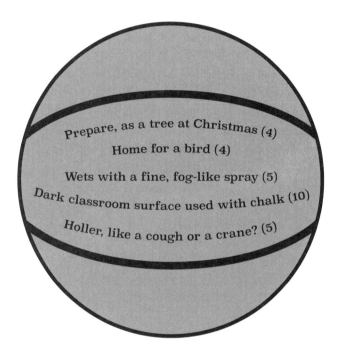

Prepare, as a tree at Christmas (4)

Home for a bird (4)

Wets with a fine, fog-like spray (5)

Dark classroom surface used with chalk (10)

Holler, like a cough or a crane? (5)

## Digits and Dragons

Ahmad, meanwhile, was freaking out about finding a Digits and Dragons machine in the corner, "I loved this game! You all remember it, right?" Everyone shook their heads. "You *have* to remember. You play an adventurer who's going through a maze fighting monsters, and you've got to collect swords and keys and go through magic portals ..." No spark of recognition was evident on anyone's face. "Whatever," Ahmad sighed. Then he spotted something that perked him up: "Hey, nice, an issue of *Video Game Quarterly*! Ooh, with a special article on Digits and Dragons strategy tips." He opened the magazine to the one page it would open to. "Looks more like a sudoku than an article about strategy tips. Too bad Juan isn't here, he'd love this. More importantly, he would solve it for me. Oh, well, who's got a pencil?" (The "strategy tips" appear on the next page.)

# Rules

To escape the dungeon you must slay all the monsters, and find a key that will unlock the door. You begin your adventure in the square containing your icon.

You can move one square at a time horizontally or vertically. You may not move diagonally. The given numbers are walls that you may not pass through; they are shaded gray. Entering a **portal** will immediately teleport you to a corresponding portal with the same number. (If there is more than one portal, you will have to determine which one corresponds with which.) You may not enter any square more than once, including portals.

You are empty-handed when you begin. To slay a **monster** you must be carrying a **sword** that is more powerful than the monster. (The power of a sword or a monster is indicated by the number on its square; higher numbers are more powerful.) You can pick up a sword by entering its square, and slay a monster by entering its square when you are carrying a powerful enough sword. (If you enter a monster's square with a weaker sword or with no sword at all, it will eat you.) You can only carry one sword at a time; slaying a monster destroys the sword. Remember, all monsters must be slain before leaving.

To leave the dungeon, you will have to unlock the **door**. To do this, you must be carrying a **key** that fits its lock. A key and door only match if their squares have the same number. Happy adventuring!

| You | Portal | Sword | Monster | Door | Key |
|-----|--------|-------|---------|------|-----|

After completing the sudoku, Ahmad noticed that the machine was showing the high score screen, and prompting him to add his initials. Above the space for the initials, these symbols appeared:

He entered ... well, not his initials, anyway ... and, in return, received a chain of prize tickets. Can you solve the sudoku and figure out what he entered?

# Tee Ceremony

Ichiko and Ewan stood staring at a locked glass case, quite grandly filled with a T-shirt display in honor of all the cities where this arcade used to have locations. "I guess 'Robot Genie's Cybercastle' must have been quite the franchise back in its day," Ichiko said, "Looks like it used to be all over the place." "You know what," Greg said, "I think there are some prize tickets tucked into one of those shirts. Let's get this case open. It looks like there's a control panel under the lock." The control panel had a keyboard and a small screen, and the screen was showing this prompt: "State what you're looking at." Greg hesitated, "What I've got is kinda long. It makes sense though ... I guess I'll try it." It worked, allowing them to retrieve more prize tickets. Can you figure out what he typed? (If you'd like a hint from Greg, see page 95. To check the password for this puzzle, check each word individually.)

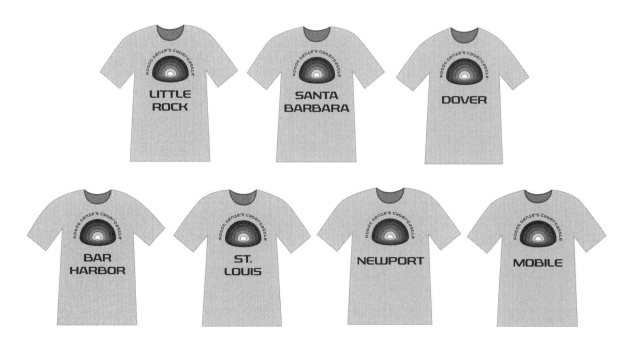

# Taking the Plunger

"Thank goodness," said Ewan, walking up to a pinball machine named Pinball Lizard. "It wouldn't feel like an arcade if there wasn't one of these." A token sat on top of the machine even though it was set to free play. Ewan gave the ball plunger a good *sproing* and played for about 30 seconds before his flipper skills failed him. On the front of the machine, next to the slot, was this set of handwritten clues in place of the usual game instructions. After studying it for a moment, he performed a sequence of actions, after which the machine flashed various lights and whatnot, and dispensed several prize tickets. Can you figure out what he did? (To check your answer to this puzzle, combine the initial letters of each instruction as a password.)

- Enlist, or fuse together (4)
- It's refracted by prisms (5)
- You fly one in the wind (4)
- The crime of stealing (5)
- Sense associated with the eyes (5)
- Satisfying weight of something in your hand (4)
- Warp's crosser, on a loom (4)
- Competitor in a joust (6)
- Pamplona pursuer (4)

# It's All Downhill From Here

In one corner of the arcade stood two skiing-themed games: a video game, Ski Pole Position, and a physical game, Ski-Ball, in which players roll a set of nine balls up a ramp into circles to score points. Ciara swooped in again, saying "Step aside, losers!," and rolled nine balls in a row into the 150 target. Nothing happened. "Argh, not again," she muttered, "This game doesn't even make sense. You ski *downhill*, not *uphill*. Let me try this other game instead." But Ski Pole Position seemed to be stuck on the high score screen. After a few moments, Ciara turned her attention back to the Ski-Ball game and rolled nine balls once again; this time, bells rang and the machine dispensed some prize tickets. What targets did she hit with her nine rolls? (To check the "combination" to this puzzle, run the scores of all nine rolls together as a single long number.)

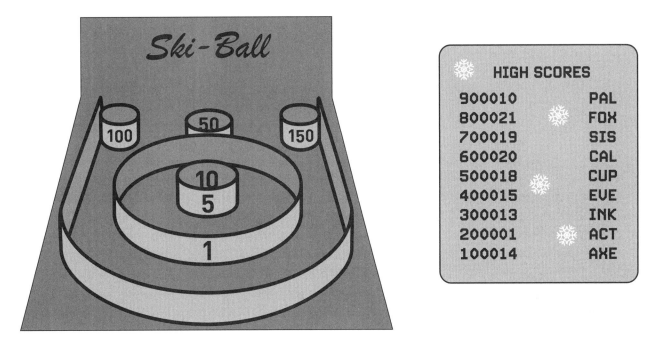

# The Long Arm of the Claw

"Oh, no, not a claw machine," Kamala groaned, "I can see there's a plastic box in there filled with prize tickets, but no one never manages to grab anything with that frickin' claw!" "I don't think we're meant to," Olga said, testing out the joystick, "The claw won't move at all. But there's an access panel on the side, with a keyboard to enter a password." "Interesting," said Kamala, "So what else is in there besides the prize tickets?" "A bunch of plush toys, and some other stuff. Let's see …" There were six stuffed toys with labels identifying them; they were an alien with green skin, a red apple, a pale yellow coyote, Ernie from *Sesame Street*, a blue heron, and Emperor Zurg from *Toy Story 2*. There were also six non-plush items: a calendar, a Game Genie, a fold-up scooter, a map of Zurich, a model Jeep Cherokee, and a stapler. After some discussion Kamala and Olga tried a password, and they were soon retrieving the box of prize tickets. Can you figure out what the password was?

# Cheat Codes

Ahmad, finished with the sudoku, wandered to a shelf and said, "Wow, this arcade even has a home video game console. Aw, yes, this one's a classic—the original Unintend-o! You remember its slogan, right? 'You'll play for hours, even if you didn't mean to.' You *must* remember it." Clearly, no one did. "Whatever," Ahmad sighed, perusing the stack of games and a sheet labeled "Cheat Codes." He couldn't find the famous "up, up, down, down, left, right, left, right, B, A, start" on it, but it had plenty of others. It didn't indicate which ones went with which game, though. The console was hooked up to an old TV; he flipped the power switch and the screen lit up with a grid of letters. Using the controller, he was able to highlight letters, and he got right to work. After solving the puzzle, Ahmad picked up the controller and entered a sequence of 8 buttons; in response, the console opened and revealed a small pile of prize tickets. What did he enter? (For a starting hint, see page 96. Following that on the same page are full instructions, and a hint to the final step.)

- CASTLEVANIA
- COMBAT
- CRAZY CLIMBER
- DOUBLE DRAGON
- EXCITEBIKE
- GALAXIAN
- GHOSTS 'N' GOBLINS
- LUNAR LANDER
- MANIAC MANSION
- MARBLE MADNESS
- METAL GEAR
- MS. PAC-MAN
- NINJA GAIDEN
- PAPERBOY
- PITFALL!
- Q*BERT
- RAMPAGE
- ROBOTRON
- SUPER MARIO BROS.

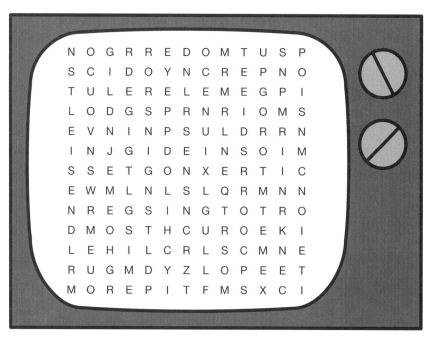

```
N O G R R E D O M T U S P
S C I D O Y N C R E P N O
T U L E R E L E M E G P I
L O D G S P R N R I O M S
E V N I N P S U L D R R N
I N J G I D E I N S O I M
S S E T G O N X E R T I C
E W M L N L S L Q R M N N
N R E G S I N G T O T R O
D M O S T H C U R O E K I
L E H I L C R L S C M N E
R U G M D Y Z L O P E E T
M O R E P I T F M S X C I
```

up, B, up, right, right, start
up, up, right, B, A, right, start
down, right, right, right, A, up, up, start
up, A, up, up, A, left, left, start
down, right, up, A, up, right, A, right, start
up, A, up, A, up, up, A, right, start
left, A, up, up, left, B, up, right, start
up, right, B, up, right, right, right, up, start
right, up, right, A, down, down, left, A, left, start
left, down, right, right, up, up, B, up, left, left, start
left, left, up, A, left, up, A, up, up, left, left, start
left, A, left, down, down, down, right, A, down, left, A, start
down, left, left, down, A, right, A, right, right, right, down, start
right, down, A, down, left, up, left, left, down, B, down, left, start
left, left, up, B, right, right, up, up, A, left, left, left, start
right, A, right, up, A, right, up, A, up, up, up, up, left, start
left, A, up, B, up, right, up, A, left, up, up, up, right, start
right, up, up, right, right, up, up, up, right, B, down, down, right, up, start
left, left, down, left, left, down, A, down, right, right, B, down, down, left, start

**CHEAT CODES**

*Don't forget the "start"!*

# Counter Intuitive

"We've got all these prize tickets," Ichiko said, "Do we get any prizes? I wouldn't mind a new fidget spinner." "Well, let's check out the prize counter," Ewan replied, "Oh, wow, there's a whole lot going on over here." The rest of the group came over, and checked out the list of prizes and the amount of tickets needed to exchange for each. "Key to back room??," Greg shouted, pointing at the last item on the list, "That's exactly what we need! How do we get it?" Kamala called back from the end of the counter, "Looks like it's automated. You feed tickets into this ticket redemption machine, select your prize, and it opens a little door so you can take it." "Well, we have 40 tickets exactly!," Greg said, "Let's get redeemin'!" "Oh, as if it would ever be that simple," Kamala said, "The machine is turned off. There's a power switch, but it's behind a locked panel. We need a password." Olga sighed, "Of course we do. Hey ... one of these prize doors is open. Looks like it's got a little phone book inside. Weird prize. It says 'Emergency Numbers,' and then it has a list of initials, but no phone numbers." "Wait!," Ewan interjected, "I remember seeing that on a board of sticky notes over by that old pay phone!" (The page from the phone book, the bulletin board, and the pay phone's keypad are all shown below.) The group studied both, then, after some brainstorming by Ciara (see page 96 if you'd like to hear her ideas), they entered the correct password. Can you figure out what it was?

| | | |
|---|---|---|
| 1 ticket | — | jacks |
| 2 tickets | — | finger trap |
| 3 tickets | — | mood ring |
| 4 tickets | — | sticky hand |
| 4 tickets | — | miniature clock |
| 5 tickets | — | toy soldier |
| 5 tickets | — | fake moustache |
| 6 tickets | — | slide whistle |
| 6 tickets | — | travel chess set |
| 7 tickets | — | pinwheel |
| 7 tickets | — | jump rope |
| 8 tickets | — | balloon animal kit |
| 9 tickets | — | glowing glasses |
| 10 tickets | — | paddle ball |
| 11 tickets | — | playing cards |
| 12 tickets | — | charm bracelet |
| 40 tickets | — | key to back room |

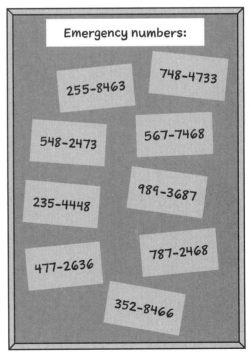

# That's the Ticket

Once the machine was reactivated, a screen lit up with instructions for how to redeem tickets: "To claim an item, simply insert the correct tickets and press the 'redeem' button on its door. For any item valued at 12 tickets or less, you may use tickets of any color; for any item with a value greater than 12 tickets, follow the rules below." "Uh-oh," said Greg, "Dare I look?" They spread out their tickets on the counter (as a reminder, they had collected 5 orange tickets, 7 blue tickets, 3 purple tickets, 8 yellow tickets, 6 silver tickets, 5 olive tickets, and 6 crimson tickets; the various tickets were all labeled with their colors), and studied the rules.

1. Tickets must be divided into exactly 15 sets, and no set may contain more than five tickets. (A "set" is any group of consecutive tickets of the same color; a set may be a single ticket.)

2. Purple tickets may not be adjacent to silver tickets in the sequence.

3. Every set of olive tickets must be preceded by the same color of ticket.

4. Ticket #22 and ticket #29 must be the first tickets of two sets that are the same length.

5. The yellow tickets must be divided into exactly two sets, separated by at least 10 other tickets.

6. Of the sets of silver tickets, exactly two must be the same length. No other color of ticket may have any sets of the same length.

7. All the orange tickets must be used before any blue tickets are used, which must all be used before any purple tickets are used.

8. No two tickets that are exactly 30 tickets apart (e.g., the 1st ticket and the 31st ticket) may be the same color.

9. One consecutive sequence of ten tickets consists of four sets of tickets—blue, crimson, olive, and silver, in some order—all of different lengths.

10. Every set of five tickets must be adjacent to a purple ticket.

11. There must be exactly as many sets of crimson tickets as there are sets of silver tickets.

12. If you divide the sequence into four groups of ten tickets (1–10, 11–20, 21–30, and 31–40), one group of ten must contain three single tickets of different colors, and seven tickets of one other color.

13. In a different group of ten (of the same sets in rule 12), there must be two separate pairs of adjacent single tickets; those two pairs are the only adjacent sets in the entire sequence of 40 that may contain the same number of tickets, and the four tickets in the two pairs must all be different colors.

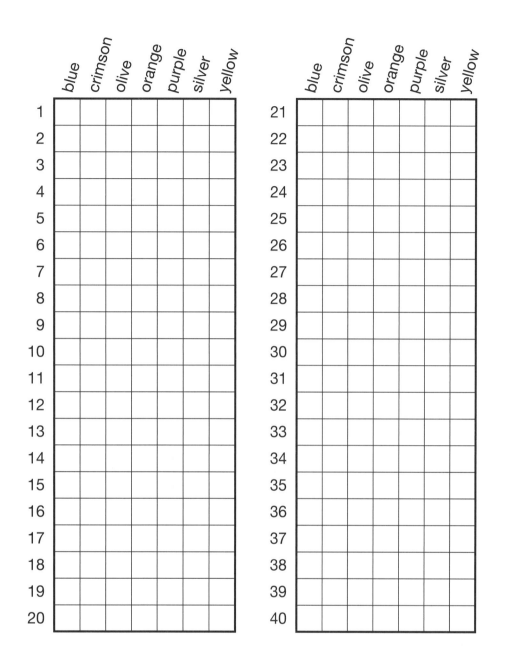

After much discussion and shuffling of tickets, they agreed that they'd found the only possible order, fed the tickets into the machine (which helpfully gave them a receipt detailing everything they had inserted), then pressed the button to redeem the key to the back room. The door popped open to reveal... "A locked box!?," Ciara shouted, "That requires a password?? No!" "Hang on, hang on," Kamala said, "I don't think there are any more puzzles left. We must be able to figure out the password from something we've already done." "Yeah!," Ewan chimed in, "And come to think of it, why ..." (To hear Ewan's observation, see page 96.) They consulted for a moment, then swiftly entered the password, retrieved the key, and swooped into the back room in triumph. (It really did contain a playable Pong machine, as well as souvenir Robot Genie's Cybercastle t-shirts for sale.) Can you reconstruct the sequence of tickets, and figure out the password?

# Epilogue

The next weekend, all 15 friends were gathered in Bette's backyard for a barbecue. "Folks," Dagmar said, "I think between us we may have solved every escape room in town." "That's true," Frieda said, "We've kind of exhausted all the options. But I think I've come up with a solution as to what we should do next. In fact, I wrote a little inspirational speech about it. Don't worry, it's short."

She stood up and read from a small note card: "We're relatively intelligent, that's evident. Now, examining weekend entertainment selections, can anything provide equal reward? Our own minds, say?" She sat back down.

"You're right, that *was* short," Heath said. Ichiko leaned over, "Hang on, can I take a look at your notes?" Frieda smiled and handed over the card. "Oh!," Ichiko laughed, "That's a great idea!" Ichiko explained to the rest of the group, who enthusiastically agreed with Ichiko's assessment, and they started discussing plans right away.

What was Frieda's idea?

# Answers & Explanations

**Page 7, top: Flipping Out**

From clue 4, we know that none of the following pairs of people had matching coin flips: Ahmad & Bette, Greg & Heath, Ewan & Ichiko, Ichiko & Juan. Since both Ewan and Juan have different coin flips from Ichiko, their coin flips are identical. Now let's consider clue 3. We know the winning escape room would have been different without the coin flips of Bette, Greg, Heath, and Juan; we also know that Greg and Heath's coin flips were different. If Bette and Juan's coin flips were also different, then Bette, Greg, Heath, and Juan would have two heads and two tails between them, which could not change the outcome. Therefore, Bette and Juan's flips were the same. (Let's call their flip X, since we don't know whether it was heads or tails, and call the opposite flip Y.) Combining that information with what we know from clue 4, we can determine that Bette, Ewan, and Juan all flipped X, and Ahmad and Ichiko flipped Y.

Since we now know Ahmad and Ewan's coin flips did not match, we know from clue 1 that Greg, Ichiko, and Kamala's flips *did* match, so Greg and Kamala also flipped Y (and since Greg and Heath's flips didn't match, Heath flipped X). Now, note that Bette, Greg, Heath, and Juan flipped X three times and Y once. Per clue 3, the other seven flips must have included more Y's than X's. But if they included five Y's and two X's, three X's and one Y would not be enough to change the outcome. Therefore, those seven flips included four Y's and three X's, and Ahmad, Ichiko, and Kamala already account for three of the Y's. Ciara and Dagmar's matching flips (per clue 5), then, must both be X's. The fourth Y, by elimination, was flipped by Frieda. Finally, we can use clue 2 to determine who flipped heads and who flipped tails: Bette, Frieda, and Kamala flipped Y twice and X once, so Y is heads and X is tails, and since tails won, the friends are headed to Shut and Open Case.

In summary: Ahmad flipped heads, Bette flipped tails, Ciara flipped tails, Dagmar flipped tails, Ewan flipped tails, Frieda flipped heads, Greg flipped heads, Heath flipped tails, Ichiko flipped heads, Juan flipped tails, and Kamala flipped heads.

**Page 7, bottom: Road Trip!**

Per clue 2, Ahmad cannot have been seated in the back of any car; per clues 1 and 3, the only person he could be seated next to is Greg. Since Greg doesn't drive (clue 5), Ahmad was one of the drivers and Greg was seated to his right.

Three people have 4-letter names, and four each have 5-letter and 6-letter names. Since every front seat was occupied (clue 1) and everyone whose names are the same length sat in different positions (clue 4), the front seats were occupied by two people each with 4-letter, 5-letter, and 6-letter names.

Who was the other 4-letter person in the front seat? If it was Juan, he could only have been paired with Bette (per clues 1 and 3), and by elimination the other pair could only have been Dagmar and Ichiko. But consider clues 2 and 3; no one could have sat behind Juan (since the only person with a name later in the alphabet is Kamala). So both seats behind Greg and Ichiko must have been occupied—but Heath can't have been seated behind Greg (per clue 3), which means Kamala is the only option for having been seated behind both Greg and Ichiko, which is impossible.

Therefore Ewan must have been in the front seat, and since Greg was in the passenger seat, Ewan was another driver. Per clue 1, Ewan can only have been seated next to Ichiko. Per clues 1 and 3 (and by elimination), in the remaining car, Bette sat in the passenger seat, and the driver was either Dagmar or Kamala. If the driver was Kamala, however, we run into a similar contradiction: no one could be seated behind Kamala, but no one could be seated behind Ichiko either (since Kamala is in the front seat of another car, and Juan can't be in Ichiko's car per clue 2). The third driver was therefore Dagmar.

Per clue 2, Frieda and Heath can't have been in Greg's car or Ewan and Ichiko's car, so they were the other two passengers in Dagmar and Bette's car. Juan can't have been in Ichiko's car, so he was in Ahmad and Greg's car. Kamala can't have been in Juan's car, so she was in Ewan and Ichiko's car. Ciara can't have been in Ewan and Ichiko's car, since her name precedes both of theirs alphabetically (clue 2), so she was in Ahmad and Greg's car, and per clue 2 must have been seated behind Ahmad, with Juan seated to her right. Heath can't have been seated in the same position as Ciara (clue 4), so he was seated on the right with Frieda to his left. Also per clue 4, Kamala can't have been in the same position as Frieda, so she was seated on the right with an empty seat to her left.

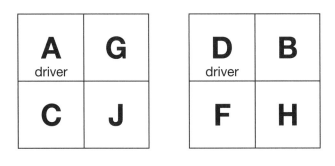

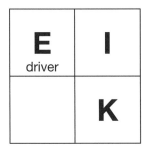

**Page 8, top: Distance Learning**

The "distances" are actually indexes into the city names, with the arrows on the sign indicating which direction to read the indexes. For instance, the "St. Petersburg" sign (labeled 836) points to the left; we take the 8th, 3rd, and 6th letters of the city, reading from right to left. The 8th letter from the right is T, the 3rd from the right is U, and the 6th from the right is R. On the sign for Milwaukee (labeled 719), we do the same, but reading from left to right. The 7th letter is K, the 1st is M, and the 9th is E. Doing the same for Nashville from right to left gives us the letters N, I, and S; finally, doing the same for Sacramento from left to right gives T, A, and N. Together, the letters spell TURKMENISTAN. Finding the country of Turkmenistan on the globe and pressing it opens the globe to reveal a red key.

**Page 8, bottom: Spark of Inspiration**

By moving three matchsticks, we can make the incorrect equation correct:

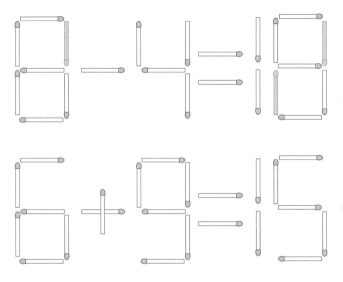

The four digits of the correct equation, 6915, are the combination to the box, which contains a blue key.

**Page 9: Wildlife**

Ciara and Heath counted the same kind of animal (clue 5). It wasn't birds, because Kamala was one of the two people who counted birds (clue 6). Frieda and Juan did not count the same kind of animal (clue 1), but neither can have counted whatever Ciara and Heath did, so either Frieda or Juan was the second person who counted birds. That means Dagmar didn't count birds, and since we know she also didn't count raccoons (clue 9), Dagmar counted squirrels. By elimination, then, Ciara and Heath must have counted raccoons.

Since Ciara counted an odd number of animals (clue 7), she wasn't counting raccoons in the north window, since the number counted there was twice as many as the number in the east window (clue 4). Therefore Ciara counted raccoons in the east window and Heath counted them in the north window. Dagmar and Kamala were at different windows (clue 2), so of the remaining two people (Frieda and Juan), one was at each window. Since Frieda was at the north window (clue 12), Juan was at the east window. The three people at the east window counted $x$, $x+3$, and $x+8$ animals (clue 12); Ciara's count was $x+3$, since she didn't count the most or least (clue 7), and since she counted an odd number of animals (clue 7), the other two people must have counted an even number. The two even numbers weren't prime (since no one counted only two animals, per clue 13), and since Heath counted twice as many animals as Ciara, Heath didn't count a prime number either. So since three people counted primes (clue 11), Ciara must have counted a prime number, as did the two people at the north window besides Heath. Since Dagmar didn't count a prime number (clue 11), she therefore must have been at the east window, and by elimination Kamala was at the north window. To sum up, then:

Frieda, Heath, and Kamala were at the north window; and Ciara, Dagmar, and Juan were at the east window. Juan counted the fewest animals overall (clue 13), so Juan counted $x$ animals, and Dagmar counted $x+8$. Since people at the same window didn't count the same type of animal, by elimination Frieda counted squirrels and Juan counted birds.

Now let's consider the maximum number of animals anyone can have counted. Everyone counted at least four animals (per clue 13, since Juan's count is even), and each number of the combination is made up of the total of four people's counts, two from each window. The lowest possible count any two people can have is $4+5=9$, so since the highest possible number of the combination is 39, no pair of people in either window can have a combined count higher than 30, since they will pair up with two people who must have counted at least nine animals.

As previously determined, Juan counted $x$ animals, Ciara counted $x+3$, and Dagmar counted $x+8$. Ciara's count was prime and at least seven or Juan would have counted too few, per clue 13. If Ciara counted 13 animals, Dagmar would have counted 18, making a total of 31, which we've already shown is impossible. If Ciara counted 11, then Dagmar would have counted 16. But Ciara will always be paired up with Heath (since they both counted raccoons), who counted twice as many raccoons as Ciara, and $11+16+22=49$, far too high for the combination lock. Ciara then, must have counted 7 raccoons. Juan counted 4 birds, Dagmar counted 12 squirrels, and Heath counted 14 raccoons.

Ciara, Dagmar, and Heath collectively counted $7+12+14=33$ raccoons and squirrels, so Frieda, who also counted squirrels, cannot have counted more than six of them. We already know she was one of the three people from clue 11 who counted a prime number; she didn't count fewer than Juan (clue 13), so she can only have counted five squirrels. Kamala was the other person who counted a prime number, and her total was the sum of two other people's counts (clue 10). She can't have counted more than 14 animals or the combined total of raccoons and birds would be too high, and the only lower prime total that is possible to make from the other five counts (4, 5, 7, 12, and 14) is 11 (4+7).

In summary, the group counted a total of 15 birds, 21 raccoons, and 17 squirrels, so the combination (calculated from the sums of bird + squirrel, squirrel + raccoon, and bird + raccoon) is $15+17$, $17+21$, $15+21$, or 32-38-36. That combination opens the box to reveal a silver key.

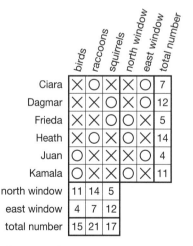

|  | birds | raccoons | squirrels | north window | east window | total number |
|---|---|---|---|---|---|---|
| Ciara | X | O | X | X | O | 7 |
| Dagmar | X | X | O | X | O | 12 |
| Frieda | X | X | O | O | X | 5 |
| Heath | X | O | X | O | X | 14 |
| Juan | O | X | X | X | O | 4 |
| Kamala | O | X | X | O | X | 11 |
| north window | 11 | 14 | 5 | | | |
| east window | 4 | 7 | 12 | | | |
| total number | 15 | 21 | 17 | | | |

**Page 10: Park It**

The cryptogram, when solved, reveals the following list of National Parks:

> YELLOWSTONE
> YOSEMITE
> GATEWAY ARCH
> JOSHUA TREE
> CRATER LAKE
> CAPITOL REEF
> GLACIER
> DEATH VALLEY
> MAMMOTH CAVE
> KENAI FJORDS
> HOT SPRINGS
> DRY TORTUGAS
> EVERGLADES

Some letters in the list have been replaced with question marks; those letters, read in order, spell ONE THREE FIVE FOUR, the combination to the box, which contains a gold key.

**Page 11: Under Log and Key**

No two people who sat in the same seat on the drive had the same role (clue 1). That means that of the three drivers (Ahmad, Dagmar, and Ewan), the three front seat passengers (Bette, Greg, and Ichiko), and the three people in the right-hand back seat (Heath, Juan, and Kamala), one per group must have been standing at the fireplace. Therefore, neither Ciara nor Frieda was at the fireplace. Additionally, per clue 2, no one who stood at the east window counting wildlife was at the fireplace, so Dagmar and Juan can also be eliminated from that position. (Ciara, the third, has already been eliminated.) Greg and Kamala were paired up at a keyhole (clue 7), so neither of them was at the fireplace either. That leaves Ahmad, Bette, Ewan, Heath, and Ichiko, and since the three people at the fireplace had names of different lengths (clue 4), Ewan and Ichiko must have been two of them. Since Ahmad was in the same car as Ewan, and Bette was in the same car as Ichiko, per clue 1 they weren't at the fireplace, so by elimination Heath was the third person at the fireplace.

Of the other eight people (Ahmad, Bette, Ciara, Dagmar, Frieda, Greg, Juan, and Kamala), we know Greg and Kamala were a pair. Per clue 2, we know that none of Ciara, Dagmar, and Juan were paired with each other. So the four pairs are Ciara + someone, Dagmar + someone, Juan + someone, and Greg + Kamala. Ahmad was not paired with Ciara or Juan, since they all sat in the same car (clue 1), so he was paired with Dagmar. Since Ahmad did not hold a key (clue 6), Dagmar did. Juan didn't lift an object (clue 3), so Kamala, who sat in the same position as Juan (clue 1), did, and since Kamala and Greg were paired up, Greg held a key. Greg sat in the same position as Bette, so Bette did not hold a key, and by elimination Ciara held a key.

Of the four people who lifted objects (Ahmad, Bette, Frieda, and Kamala), only one was a man, so Ahmad lifted the statue (clue 5). The silver key was held by a woman, so of the four people who had keys (Ciara, Dagmar, Greg, or Juan), it must have been held by Ciara or Dagmar. But the silver key and statue were not a pair, and Ahmad was paired with Dagmar, so Ciara held the silver key. Of the remaining people with keys, only Juan had been in the back

seat, so he held the red key, and he wasn't paired with Bette, who sat in the front seat, so he was paired with Frieda (who lifted the lamp, per the instructions), and by elimination Ciara was paired with Bette. Greg didn't have the gold key (clue 7), so by elimination he held the blue key and Dagmar held the gold key. The blue key was not paired with the umbrella stand (clue 9), so by elimination Kamala lifted the record player and Bette lifted the umbrella stand. In summary: Ahmad lifted the statue for Dagmar's gold key; Bette lifted the umbrella stand for Ciara's silver key; Frieda lifted the lamp for Juan's red key; Kamala lifted the record player for Greg's blue key; Ewan, Heath & Ichiko moved the fireplace.

**Page 12: Bio Engineering**

The names of the biographies' subjects each contain a three-letter sequence of letters that are alphabetically adjacent:

> agameMNOn
> dante aliGHIeri
> cAB Calloway
> oscar hammeRSTein
> DEForest kelley
> dylan mCDErmott
> john STUart mill
> friedrich wilheLM Nietzsche
> luciaNO Pavarotti

Alphabetizing the names by those sets of three letters gives the following order:

> ABC: Cab Calloway • •
> CDE: Dylan McDermott • /
> DEF: DeForest Kelley – /
> GHI: Dante Alighieri – –
> LMN: Friedrich Wilhelm Nietzsche – /
> MNO: Agamemnon • –
> NOP: Luciano Pavarotti • /
> RST: Oscar Hammerstein – •
> STU: John Stuart Mill – –

Now that the books are in the right order, the symbols on the stickers read:

$$\bullet \bullet \bullet / - / - - - / \bullet - \bullet / - \bullet - -$$

This is, indeed, Morse code, with the slashes indicating breaks between letters. It translates to the word STORY, the password that opens the safe, revealing a book within: *Marjorie Morningstar*, by Herman Wouk.

**Page 13, top: Playing Tags**

If you try to solve the sudoku with only the given letters, you will soon see that it's impossible to make much progress. The first step, then, is to figure out where the names can be placed. For instance, where can DIEGO fit? We can eliminate rows and columns where there obviously isn't room for it (like row 1 and row 5, where the D is too far to the right). In many rows and columns where there is room for the name, placing it would cause a contradiction (for instance, writing it in row 2 would cause there to be two I's in the third column, while writing it in column 8 would cause there to be two G's in the upper right box). As it happens, there's only one place to put it: in row 7, in the five empty spaces to the left of the L. Below is what the grid looks like after writing it in, and filling in all the letters that can now be deduced.

With the new information, there's now only one place where DEL will fit, which lets us solve more of the grid, getting us here:

Now there's only one place for ROD and LENI to fit, and once those are placed, NEIL's position is also narrowed down to one spot. After filling those in and continuing to solve, we just have a few empty squares remaining on the right side of the grid.

Our last name that's left to be placed will only fit in the rightmost column, and placing it allows us to complete the puzzle. In the completed grid, reading along the long diagonal from upper left to lower right, is the librarian's recommendation for escapist reading: *Gone Girl*, by Gillian Flynn, which Ewan found hidden in plain sight, in a nearby stack of books.

### Page 13, bottom: Little Blank Books

The ten words can be placed in the blanks to make five book titles, with extra letters in each of the placed words:

*The Lay of the Land* (The **P**LAY of the LAN**ED**) by Richard Ford
*The Art of War* (The **W**ART of WAR**T**) by Sun Tzu
*Hard Times* (**H**EARD TIM**ERS**) by Charles Dickens
*Light in August* (**P**LIGHT in AUGUST**A**) by William Faulkner
*All My Rage* (**W**ALL My RA**N**GE) by Sabaa Tahir

The extra letters, in order, read PEWTER PAWN. Once again deleting one letter from each word, we get another book title, *Peter Pan*, by J.M. Barrie, which is the book that Dagmar found.

### Page 14, top: Dewey or Don't We?

First things first: did you come up with the combination 53769? If so, that doesn't open the lock; if you'd like to keep trying, don't read on.

Using the poster, we can classify the five books like so:

*F=ma: The Most Important Equation* (500–599: Mathematics, Physics, Chemistry, and Biology)
*How to Avoid Self-Incrimination in Court* (300–399: Sociology and Law)
*Playing the Hot Corner* (700–799: Arts, Recreation, and Sports)
*Recipes for your Independence Day Celebration* (600–699: Applied Science [inventions, transportation, cookbooks])
*The Battle of the Somme* (900–999: Geography and History)

Taking the first number of the classification for each book gives us 53769—which, as noted above, does not open the lock, so there's another step to figure out. Looking more closely at the subjects of the books shows that they have something interesting in common. "F=ma" is Newton's second law of motion. Avoiding self-incrimination is the subject of the fifth amendment. The "hot corner" in baseball is third base. Independence Day is July 4th, and the Battle of the Somme happened in the First World War.

Ordering the five books in the order "first, second, third, fourth, fifth" according to their subjects, and reading off the first digits of their Dewey Decimal classifications, we then get the combination 95763, which opens the lock to reveal the book *Silent Spring*, by Rachel Carson.

**Pages 14–15: Shelf-Help Group**

The four books are *Gone Girl* by Gillian Flynn, *Marjorie Morningstar* by Herman Wouk, *Peter Pan* by J.M. Barrie, and *Silent Spring* by Rachel Carson.

Of the four books, the only one that fits the description in clue 3 is *Peter Pan*; replacing the initial letters in its title with the M's of *Marjorie Morningstar* makes "meter" and "man." *Peter Pan*, then, was on the top shelf of one of the bookshelves, and *Marjorie Morningstar* was on the east wall.

The book on the west wall was either *Gone Girl* or *Silent Spring* (clue 8), so *Peter Pan* was on the north or south wall. However, if *Silent Spring* were on the west wall, then *Gone Girl* and *Peter Pan* would have to be opposite each other on the north and south walls. This is impossible, though, since *Peter Pan* and *Gone Girl* have the same number of letters and must be placed on adjacent walls (clue 10). *Gone Girl*, therefore, was placed on the west wall.

It's possible to swap two books so that the titles are alphabetized either in order from top to bottom or from bottom to top (clue 4). We know *Peter Pan* is on the top shelf, which is not its correct alphabetized position in either direction. There are, therefore, only two possible orders in which the books can be shelved from top to bottom, since *Peter Pan* will need to be one of the two books that swaps positions; it will swap to its correct position with a book that should go in the position *Peter Pan* occupies, with the other two books correctly placed. This means the order from top to bottom must be either *Peter Pan, Marjorie Morningstar, Gone Girl, Silent Spring* (in which case *Peter Pan* and *Gone Girl* can be swapped to alphabetize the books from top to bottom); or *Peter Pan, Silent Spring, Marjorie Morningstar, Gone Girl* (in which case *Peter Pan* and *Silent Spring* can be swapped to alphabetize the books from bottom to top). However, the books on the two lowest shelves weren't across from each other (clue 5), and since we know *Gone Girl* is on the west wall and *Marjorie Morningstar* is on the east wall, they can't be the two lowest books. The order from top to bottom, therefore, is *Peter Pan, Marjorie Morningstar, Gone Girl, Silent Spring*.

Ahmad stood on the top step, and his book was on the lowest shelf (clue 6). We now know *Silent Spring* was on the lowest shelf, and we've narrowed it down to being on either the north or south wall. But since Dagmar stood on the north ladder (clue 7), Ahmad stood on the south ladder to place *Silent Spring*, and *Peter Pan* was on the north wall. The people on the two lowest ladder positions stood opposite each other (clue 5), so they were on the west and east ladders in some order, and by elimination Dagmar was standing on the third step of the north ladder. Of the remaining two people, since Ewan was on a higher step than Ichiko (clue 9), Ewan stood on the second step and Ichiko stood on the bottom step. Since the shelf and ladder step never matched along any wall (clue 2), Ewan wasn't the one who placed *Gone Girl* on the second shelf of the west wall, so he was on the east ladder and Ichiko was on the west ladder. In summary:

On the north wall, Dagmar stood on the third step to place *Peter Pan* on the top shelf.
On the east wall, Ewan stood on the second step to place *Marjorie Morningstar* on the third shelf.
On the south wall, Ahmad stood on the top step to place *Silent Spring* on the bottom shelf.
On the west wall, Ichiko stood on the bottom step to place *Gone Girl* on the second shelf.

**Page 16: Saturday Sundaes**

The shared initial among Malik's ingredients (clue 3) can only be C, so he did not select strawberry rhubarb, peppermint watermelon, hot fudge, or diced almonds. He did not have cinnamon maple, because, per clue 7, the only person who ordered that also ordered diced almonds, which Malik didn't have, so Malik's two ice cream flavors were vanilla coriander and chocolate habanero.

Now let's consider clue 2. The ingredients with words in alphabetical order are chocolate habanero, cinnamon maple, peppermint watermelon, crushed pineapple, and butterscotch chips. The only person who ordered cinnamon maple also ordered diced almonds (clue 7), so cinnamon maple can't have been part of the all-alphabetical order, which means one person ordered chocolate habanero, peppermint watermelon, crushed pineapple, and butterscotch chips. No two people ordered the same toppings, so Malik didn't also order both crushed pineapple and butterscotch chips, and must have ordered whipped cream. The ingredients with words *not* in alphabetical order are vanilla coriander, strawberry rhubarb, hot fudge, diced almonds, and whipped cream. Since the all-not-alphabetical order must include vanilla coriander, and no one who ordered that flavor ordered diced almonds (clue 5), we know that one person ordered vanilla coriander, strawberry rhubarb, hot fudge, and whipped cream.

We've now accounted for at least part of three people's orders. The sundae in clue 7 must belong to a fourth person, since it doesn't match Malik's order or either of the orders from clue 2. None of those three sundaes include both peppermint watermelon and hot fudge, so they are not the sundae mentioned in clue 9. The sundae in clue 7 also can't be the same sundae as the one in clue 9, since only one sundae included cinnamon maple and the clue 9 sundae's other ingredient was ordered by exactly one other person. That other ingredient wasn't vanilla cardamom (which were in Malik's and the not-alphabetic sundae) or chocolate habanero (which were in Malik's and the alphabetic sundae), so it was strawberry rhubarb, and since that flavor is in the not-alphabetical sundae, it's not in any others. So it's not the other ice cream in clue 7's sundae, and neither is vanilla cardamom (which was in only two sundaes per clue 5, and we know it was in Malik's and the not-alphabetical sundae), nor peppermint watermelon (in the alphabetical sundae and clue 9's sundae, and no others per clue 9), so by elimination its other flavor is chocolate habanero.

Lily had no ingredients in common with Malik (clue 11), so she had no sundae with vanilla cardamom or chocolate habanero, and can only have had the clue 9 sundae, which so far we know contains strawberry rhubarb, peppermint watermelon, and hot fudge (and not whipped cream, since Malik and the not-alphabetic sundae include it, which contradicts clue 9). Of the remaining sundaes not yet accounted for, Olga did not order the one with cinnamon maple (clue 7) or the one with hot fudge and whipped cream (both of which were ordered by at least one other person, contradicting clue 4), so Olga was the one who had the alphabetical sundae. Kamala's sundae had an ice cream flavor in common with Lily (clue 8), and of the two sundaes remaining, only the not-alphabetical sundae has such a flavor (strawberry rhubarb); by elimination, Nelson's sundae is the one with chocolate habanero, cinnamon maple, and diced almonds.

One of Olga's toppings was ordered by no one else, but it wasn't butterscotch chips (clue 10), so she was the only one to order crushed pineapple, and by elimination, Malik's other ingredient was butterscotch chips. Crushed pineapple was the only ingredient only ordered by one person (clue 10), so someone else must have ordered diced almonds, and that can only have been Lily. Nelson's other ingredient was one he had in common with Kamala (clue 8), but it wasn't hot fudge (which was ordered by Kamala and Lily and, per clue 9, no one else), so by elimination it was whipped cream. In summary:

Kamala ordered vanilla coriander ice cream, strawberry rhubarb ice cream, hot fudge, and whipped cream.
Lily ordered strawberry rhubarb ice cream, peppermint watermelon ice cream, hot fudge, and diced almonds.
Malik ordered vanilla coriander ice cream, chocolate habanero ice cream, butterscotch chips, and whipped cream.
Nelson ordered chocolate habanero ice cream, cinnamon maple ice cream, diced almonds, and whipped cream.
Olga ordered chocolate habanero ice cream, peppermint watermelon ice cream, crushed pineapple, and butterscotch chips.

## Page 17: Oh, Grate

There were three consecutive scores, the middle one of which was equal to the number of points on one of the screws (clue 4). Which number could the middle score be? Not 2 (a score of 1 is impossible), not 3 or 5 (a score of 4 is impossible), not 7 (a score of 6 is impossible), and not 11 (while scores of 10 and 12 are possible, the only way to make each is 3+7 and 5+7, and 7 can only be in one person's score). Lily, therefore, scored 13, 17, or 19.

If Lily scored 13, two other people scored 12 and 14, which can only be made with combinations of 5+7 and 3+11. That leaves three unclaimed screws: 2, 17, and 19. For Kamala to have unscrewed two corner screws, she would have had to have a score of 19 (2+17)—but then that leaves the last 19-point screw as a singleton, giving two people scores of 19, which contradicts clue 12. Lily, then, did not score 13.

If Lily scored 17, two other people scored 16 and 18. A score of 16 can be made with 3+13 or 5+11, and a score of 18 can be made with 5+13 or 7+11. The only pair of these that uses four different screwdrivers is 3+13 and 7+11. Kamala's pair of corner screws could then only be 2+5, with the 19-point screw left over; the five scores would then be 7, 16, 17, 18, and 19. No two of these scores are five points apart, contradicting clue 3, so Lily did not score 17 either and must have scored 19.

Since Lily scored 19, two other people scored 18 and 20. A score of 18 can be made with 5+13 or 7+11, and a score of 20 can be made with 3+17 or 7+13. There are two possibilities that use four different screwdrivers: 5+13 and 3+17, or 7+11 and 3+17. For the first option, Kamala's corner pair must be 2+11=13, with the 7 left over. For the second option, Kamala's corner pair must be 2+5=7, with the 13 left over. In each case, the five scores are 7, 13,

18, 19, and 20. Malik and Nelson's scores can only be 13 and 18 respectively, per clue 3, so Kamala did not score 13 and instead scored 7, and by elimination Olga scored 20. In summary:

Olga found the 3-point and 17-point screwdrivers and went through the crawlspace first.
Lily found the 19-point screwdriver and went through the crawlspace second.
Nelson found the 7-point and 11-point screwdrivers and went through the crawlspace third.
Malik found the 13-point screwdriver and went through the crawlspace fourth.
Kamala found the 2-point and 5-point screwdrivers and went through the crawlspace last.

## Page 18–19: X Marks the Spot

The journal contains 50 capitalized five-letter words and phrases; those 50 words can be combined to construct five word squares that fit onto the five mostly blank maps. There are many ways to approach solving the word squares, but one approach is to look for the rarest letters. The letters B and J, for instance, each appear twice only, so JAMBO must intersect with JAWED and BRETT, and only one word begins with W, so WAVES intersects JAWED. There's only one option remaining for each of the rest of the words in the square (AGAVE, AGORA, DEETS, EVITE, MOVIE, and OASES), so we can finish filling in that square and move on.

The letter F also appears twice only, so FATES and FLITS must intersect. The only pair of words starting with A and L that share a letter in the second position are AUDRA and LURCH. That narrows down the possibilities for the rest of the grid entries to six (ECHO'S, IDAHO, SASSE, SHONE, TRAYS, TRY ON), which are easily filled in.

Having used four of the words with V's in them, only two remain, which must intersect: UVEAS and VITAL. UVEAS doesn't intersect U-TURN (since no words start with TI-), so it intersects USURP. The other words intersecting USURP can only be SILTY, RADIO, and PLEAD, which, once we've filled them in, make ELUDE, ATRIA, and SYNOD reading the other direction.

Two of the words with W's have been used, leaving only two remaining: DOWSE and TWIST. They must cross, and the only word with a D in the second position is ADELA, so it crosses DOWSE. The other words crossing ADELA and TWIST can only be ANTED, ANTSY, ELISA, and LASER, though we must check the crossing words to see in which order to place ANTED and ANTSY. When correctly placed, the words in the other direction are NOLAN, ESSES, and DEARY.

The remaining words are ENACT, HASN'T, ITEMS, LATEN, OPERA, PAPUA, RERAN, SLOSH, SPIRE, and SUMAC. The words ITEMS and SUMAC must cross at the M, which leaves SLOSH and SPIRE to intersect at the upper left square (with SLOSH crossing SUMAC and SPIRE crossing ITEMS). The rest of the words are then easily placed.

The next step is to figure out which grids go in which map. Each 5×5 grid could be in one of two possible orientations (with the grid flipped along the upper left–to–lower right diagonal), so we must consider ten possible grids. (The solution continues on the next page.)

The ten possible grid layouts are:

Only the JAWED grid has an E in the third position of the fourth row, and only the SPIRE grid has a U in the second position of the fourth row, so the JAWED grid must go in map 4 and the SPIRE grid must go in map 5. With the JAWED grid eliminated, only the USURP grid has an E in the fifth position of the third row, so that grid goes with map 2. That eliminates the UVEAS grid, which leaves only one grid with an A in the second position of the fourth row: the ANTED grid, which must go with map 3. Finally, the FATES grid goes in map 1, so these are the five correctly oriented grids in order:

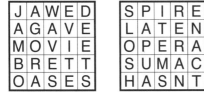

Now what? The title of the puzzle, "X Marks the Spot," gives a hint: each grid contains a letter that can be changed to an X to make two new words: FATES & TRAYS become FAXES & X-RAYS; ELUDE & SILTY become EXUDE & SIXTY; LASER & TWIST become LAXER & TWIXT; MOVIE & WAVES become MOXIE & WAXES; and LATEN & ENACT become LATEX & EXACT.

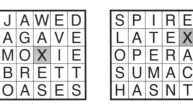

Now, we take the map on the chest and highlight the squares that correspond to those X's; reading those letters, in order from map 1's square to map 5's square, spells the combination: PATCH. Unlocking the chest and opening it reveals a distinctive bejeweled eyepatch.

## Page 20: X Marks the Spot Again

Several cages' operations can be determined right away. There are three cages with two cells whose clue is 9. Those can't be multiplication clues because the two possible products are 3×3 (which repeats a number in the same row or column) and 1×9 (which isn't possible because the highest digit in the grid is 7). Those are therefore all addition clues, as are the two cells with clues of 11 and 17, which are prime numbers and only have factors of 1 and themselves. As for the five-cell cage with the 18 clue, if it were a 18× clue, its multiplication would have to be 1×1×2×3×3 or 1×1×1×3×6. With its row of four cells, it's impossible to avoid having two identical cells in a row with those digits, so it must also be an addition clue. The two-cell cage with a 14 clue in the top row must be a multiplication clue, because the only way to make a sum of 14 with the digits 1 to 7 is 7+7, which is impossible, so that cage's multiplication is 2×7 and thus contains the digits 2 and 7 in some order. The three-cell cage with a 25 clue must also be a multiplication clue, since it's impossible to reach a number that high in a sum of three digits that are all 7 or below. Its multiplication can only be 1×5×5, with the 1 at the vertex of the

L shape and the 5's at the ends, so they don't share a row or column. The 15 clue in the nearby two-cell cage must be a 15× clue (again, the total is too high for a grid with a highest digit of 7) with a product of 3×5, which can be filled in since a 5 is already present in the fourth column. At right is the grid so far.

**66**

The 11+ cage's addition can't be 5+6 (5 is in the row already), so it's 4+7 in some order. As for the 17+ cage, there is only one way to make that sum without repeating a digit: 4+6+7. The top digit must be 6, since the third row contains 4 and 7 already. What about the cage in the upper left corner with the 15 clue? Is it addition or multiplication? We already know the totals of three cages in the top two rows; the 18+ cage, the 9+ cage, and the 14× cage (whose digits total 9). If the 15 cage is a 15+ cage, that would give us a total so far of 18+9+9+15=51 in the top two rows. Each row has a total sum of 1+2+3+4+5+6+7=28, so the top two rows together add up to 56. A count of 51 would mean that the last two cells in the second row must add up to 5—either a 1 and 4, or a 2 and 3. Those cells are part of a cage with a 14 clue; with either of those pairs of digits placed in it, it's impossible to complete the cage. If the clue is 14+, the last cell would have to be 9, which is impossible; but the clue couldn't be 14×, since neither 3 or 4 is a factor of 14. The upper left cage's clue, then, is 15× with a multiplication of 1×3×5. Those digits add up to 9, so we have a running total in the top two rows of 18+9+9+9=45, leaving a total of 11 (56−45) for the last two cells in the second row—which can be a combination of 4 and 7, or 5 and 6. In either case, the 14 clue must be an addition clue, and the third cell in the cage is 3. By elimination, the last digit in the third row is 2.

| 15× | 14× 2/7 | 2/7 | | 18+ | | 9+ |
|---|---|---|---|---|---|---|
| | | | | | | 14+ |
| 17+ 6 | 11+ 4/7 | 4/7 | 25× 5 | 1 | 3 | 24 2 |
| 4/7 | 8 | 9+ | | 5 | | |
| 4/7 | | 15× 5 | 3 | 9+ | | |
| 15 | | | 16 | | 21 | |
| 15 | | | | | | |

What about the five-cell cage with the 24 clue? Can it be an addition clue? Let's try the same analysis with the middle three rows. Three rows total 28×3=84. We know the totals of the three addition cages, the two filled-in multiplication cages (8 and 11), and the single 3 cell, and 17+11+9+8+11+3+24=83. Obviously the three remaining cells add up to more than 1, so this is impossible. The five-cell cage's clue, then, is 24×, with possible multiplications of 1×1×2×3×4 and 1×1×2×2×6. Since both of those eliminate all 1's in the last two columns, the lower right cell's clue must be 21+ (and not 21×, which would have a multiplication of 1×1×3×7). With that information, we can add together the three addition cages in the last two columns: 9+14+21=44, which means the digits in the 24× must add up to 56−44=12, which is only the case for 1×1×2×2×6. The center three rows, then, have a running total of 17+11+9+8+11+3+12=71, and so the other three squares add up to 84−71=13. The 8 cage's contents will add up to an even number no matter what (either it's an 8+ clue or it's an 8× clue containing 2×4, totaling 6), so the fifth cell in row 5 must be an odd number. It can't be 1, 3, or 5 (which appear in either the same row or column), so that cell contains a 7, and the cell below is a 2. The 8 cage must be 8×, containing 2 and 4 in some order, which fixes the placement of the digits in the 11+ cage above.

| 15× | 14× 2/7 | 2/7 | | 18+ | | 9+ |
|---|---|---|---|---|---|---|
| | | | | | | 14+ |
| 17+ 6 | 11+ 7 | 4 | 25× 5 | 1 | 3 | 24× 2 |
| 4/7 | 8× 2/4 | 9+ | | 5 | 1/2 | 1/6 |
| 4/7 | 2/4 | 15× 5 | 3 | 9+ 7 | 1/2 | 1/6 |
| 15 | | | 16 | 2 | 21+ | |
| 15 | | | | | | |

The 7 in row 5 resolves all the ambiguous digits in rows 4 and 5, and then we can fill in the 9+ cage with 3+6, in that order, by elimination. Now look at the first column. Where is the 2? It's not in the 15× cage at the top, nor in row 6 (which has a 2 in it) so it's in the bottom cell, and that cage's clue must be 15+, with 6 and 7 in the other two cells, in that order, which resolves the 14× cage in the top row. The 15 cage in row six must be a 15× cage (or the total in the bottom two rows would be too high), and its multiplication will be 1×3×5 with digits totaling 9. The 16 cage cannot be a 16+ cage for the same reason, and is a 16× cage. Its multiplication could be 1×4×4 or 2×2×4, but the 2's are all accounted for in the bottom two rows, so it's 1×4×4, with the 1 at the vertex of the L shape. By elimination, the last two cells of the bottom row are 5 and 3, in that order; the two cells above it must be 6 and 7, in that order. The 9+ cage in the upper right can now only contain 4+5 from left to right, with 7 and 4 in the 14+ cage below, by elimination.

| 15× | 14× 2 | 7 | 18+ | | 9+ 4 | 5 |
|---|---|---|---|---|---|---|
| | | | | | 14+ 7 | 4 |
| 17+ 6 | 11+ 7 | 4 | 25× 5 | 1 | 3 | 24× 2 |
| 7 | 8× 4 | 9+ 3 | 6 | 5 | 2 | 1 |
| 4 | 2 | 15× 5 | 3 | 9+ 7 | 1 | 6 |
| 15× | | | 16× 4 | 2 | 21+ 6 | 7 |
| 15+ 2 | 6 | 7 | 1 | 4 | 5 | 3 |

In the upper left 15× cage, the 5 must be in the second row. with the 1 and 3 in some order above it. In the sixth row, only the second cell can contain a 5, and the third cell can only contain a 1, so the 3 is in the first cell, and at this point everything else can be easily filled in by elimination. (There are, of course, multiple ways of approaching the puzzle, so your solving path may be different.)

| 15× 1 | 3 | 14× 2 | 7 | 18+ 6 | 9+ 4 | 5 |
|---|---|---|---|---|---|---|
| 5 | 1 | 6 | 2 | 3 | 14+ 7 | 4 |
| 17+ 6 | 11+ 7 | 4 | 25× 5 | 1 | 3 | 24× 2 |
| 7 | 8× 4 | 9+ 3 | 6 | 5 | 2 | 1 |
| 4 | 2 | 15× 5 | 3 | 9+ 7 | 1 | 6 |
| 15× 3 | 5 | 1 | 16× 4 | 2 | 21+ 6 | 7 |
| 15+ 2 | 6 | 7 | 1 | 4 | 5 | 3 |

To find the combination, bearing in mind the clue "X Marks the Spot," we look at the cells with X's—that is, ×'s. The numerical clues that are multiplication clues, reading left to right line by line, are 15×, 14×, 25×, 24×, 8×, 15×, 15×, and 16×. Using those numbers as an alphabetic cipher (A=1, B=2, C=3, etc.), they spell the phrase ONYX HOOP, the combination to the chest, which contains a round onyx (clip-on) earring.

### Page 21: X's Continue to Mark Spots

The first thing to note is that after reaching the fourth treasure and heading to the rowboat, it's still possible to retrieve either of the other treasures that connect to a cove (clue 4). This means those treasures haven't been visited yet, since each treasure can only be visited once (clue 1), so none of the first three treasures in the route are treasure 0, 5, or 9.

(The solution continues on the next page.)

Let's look at the possibilities for each of the "cove" treasures. Treasure 9 has the fewest paths leading to it, so that seems like a good place to start. If the treasure preceding treasure 9 is treasure 6, there is only one possible route that doesn't pass through treasure 5: 8-7-6-9. From there, however, it's possible to find paths that visit all the remaining treasures from either cove, which contradicts clue 4, so this is not the correct route. In the other direction, the only route that avoids treasures 0 and 5 is 2-4-3-9. This is a possibility, since there are two routes that visit all remaining treasures after rowing to treasure 0 (0-1-5-6-7-8 and 0-1-5-8-7-6), and none from treasure 5.

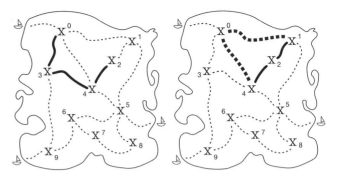

We have, then, identified seven possible routes:

- 2-4-3-9-0-1-5-6-7-8
- 2-4-3-9-0-1-5-8-7-6
- 4-2-1-5-0-3-9-6-7-8
- 1-2-4-5-0-3-9-6-7-8
- 2-4-3-0-9-6-7-8-5-1
- 1-2-4-0-5-8-7-6-9-3
- 4-2-1-0-5-8-7-6-9-3

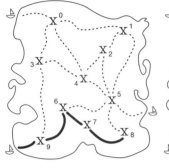 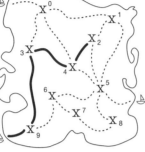

What if treasure 5 is the fourth treasure? There are fewer routes leading to it than there may seem. Since the route leading there doesn't visit treasure 9, if the preceding treasure is either treasure 6 or treasure 8, the paths are essentially the same: 6-7-8-5 or 8-7-6-5, In either case, it's possible to visit all remaining treasures from either cove, so these can be eliminated.

In the other direction, not only can the route not pass through treasure 0 or 9, it also can't pass through treasure 3. Why? Because a path like 3-4-2-5 divides the island in two, making it impossible to visit every treasure no matter which cove is visited next. This means the only possibilities in this direction are 4-2-1-5 and 1-2-4-5; from there, a complete circuit cannot be completed from treasure 9, but from treasure 0, the path continues 0-3-9-6-7-8.

In only one of these routes is there a path connecting the third and last treasures: 1-2-4-0-5-8-7-6-9-3, which is the combination that opens the frame, revealing a hidden cubbyhole containing a pirate hat and a false beard.

**Pages 22–23: Polly Gone**

The 15 busts are labeled with blanks that correspond to the names of the busts on the shelf, except there are only 14 busts on the shelf, so there is an extra one; since there are multiple people with each possible name length, we will need to use other information to figure out which is which. Correctly answering the clues on each bust gives us this list of words (from left to right, row by row): MERIT, IMPROV, PARROT, DENG, POTENT, PESTO, INGEST, LESSEN, DALI, DECADE, CHIN, RUN-ON, ATINGLE, LET UP, and MAP.

Correctly answering the sets of "Left" and "Right" clues give us these lists (in clue order):

Left: LIBERAL, BRUNO, DANGLE, SPAR, PHARMA, PRIDE, MADDEN, HOME, USING, DRAPES, BOATING, BRANCH, CHIMP, DESPOT, and BEYOND.

Right: ROVER, ROTTING, TUPELO, LENO, ESSENCE, ENTREE, RITZIER, ESTHER, TOKE, INDY, CADENCE, GONNA (from "Never Gonna Give You Up"), PRELL, NECK, and ALICE.

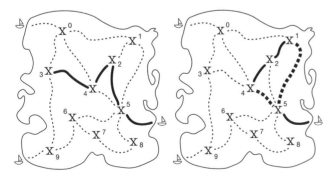

Finally, let's try treasure 0 in the fourth position. Its only possibilities that don't visit treasures 5 and 9 are 2-4-3-0 and the essentially equivalent 1-2-4-0 and 4-2-1-0. Both options work: from 2-4-3-0, the only way to complete the route is 9-6-7-8-5-1; from 1-2-4-0 or 4-2-1-0, the only option is 5-8-7-6-9-3.

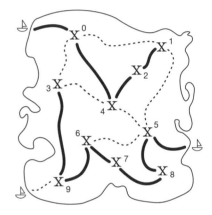

The answers to the Left and Right clues can be paired up so that, in their center, they form one of the answers to the clues on the busts, with the letters on the outside spelling the name of one of the musicians whose busts are on the shelf. For instance BRUNO and NECK combine to make B(RUNON)ECK, with RUN-ON inside BECK—and, sure enough, there are four blanks for Beck's name on the bust with the clue for RUN-ON. Here are the pairings for the rest of the given names:

BEYOND + ALICE = DALI in BEYONCE
BOATING + LENO = ATINGLE in BONO
BRANCH + INDY = CHIN in BRANDY
CHIMP + ROVER = IMPROV in CHER
DANGLE + TUPELO = LET UP in D'ANGELO
DESPOT + ENTREE = POTENT in DES'REE
DRAPES + TOKE = PESTO in DRAKE
HOME + RITZIER = MERIT in HOZIER
LIBERAL + ESSENCE = LESSEN in LIBERACE
MADDEN + GONNA = DENG in MADONNA
PHARMA + PRELL = MAP in PHARRELL
PRIDE + CADENCE = DECADE in PRINCE
USING + ESTHER = INGEST in USHER

The answers SPAR and ROTTING are left over to be paired up with the unused clue on a bust with a five-letter name: "the bird you might be trying to find." Together, SPAR + ROTTING make PARROT inside STING, which suggests to the group that there must be a bust of Sting hidden somewhere in the room, with the parrot in it. They found the bust out of sight on top of one of the bookshelves, pushed all the way back against the wall. The bust could be opened to reveal a stuffed parrot toy inside, which could be attached to one's shoulder with the use of a magnet.

**Page 24: Passphrase Reminder**

Let's take the instructions one by one. First: "Write down the eight-letter phrase that was the answer to the calcu-doku puzzle." That was ONYX HOOP:

ONYXHOOP

"Reverse that, then, at the end, add the five-letter combination to the puzzle with the 5×5 squares." That combination was PATCH:

POOHXYNOPATCH

"Find the name of a famous bear, and add the musician from the missing bust before its last letter." The famous bear is POOH, and the missing bust (which contained the parrot) was STING:

POOSTINGHXYNOPATCH

"X marks the spot; change the letter X to the Roman numeral equivalent of the three-digit number you get when you take the 3rd, 4th, and 5th digits from the combination to the map puzzle in the wooden frame." The combination was 1-2-4-0-5-8-7-6-9-3, and the 3rd, 4th, and 5th digits make the number 405, which is CDV in Roman numerals:

POOSTINGHCDVYNOPATCH

"Find a sequence of three alphabetically consecutive letters and swap the positions of the first two." There are several two-letter alphabetical sequences, but only one that is three letters long, which is NOP:

POOSTINGHCDVYONPATCH

"Find a doubled letter and change both letters to the last vowel that appears in the string." The only doubled letter is OO, which we change to AA:

PAASTINGHCDVYONPATCH

"Move the thirteenth letter to the end." The thirteenth letter is the Y:

PAASTINGHCDVONPATCHY

"Move the twelfth letter to the beginning." The twelfth letter is the V:

VPAASTINGHCDONPATCHY

"Add a W somewhere in the string to make a synonym for 'memorized.'" Adding a W after the O makes the phrase DOWN PAT:

VPAASTINGHCDOWNPATCHY

"Delete the first and last letter of the synonym you just spelled." So, we remove the D and T of DOWN PAT:

VPAASTINGHCOWNPACHY

"Find a chemical element and delete everything but its first letter." We delete everything but the T of TIN:

VPAASTGHCOWNPACHY

"Delete every G and H." That gives us:

VPAASTCOWNPACY

"Find a farm animal, and replace its last letter with the title given to a knight." The farm animal is a COW, and we change the W to the word SIR:

VPAASTCOSIRNPACY

"Reverse the first three letters and delete the middle letter of the three." The VPA becomes APV, then we delete the P in the middle:

AVASTCOSIRNPACY

"Take the eleventh and twelfth letters and place them around the center letter." The eleventh and twelfth letters are the N and P, and the center letter is the second S. For our final step, we move the N and P to surround that S and are left with the passphrase:

AVAST CONSPIRACY

… and an "avast conspiracy" is a punny way to describe the scheme that trapped you there. (Or maybe it's "a vast con's piracy"?)

**Page 25: Going Overboard**

The key to this puzzle is to look only at one type of piece at a time. The pieces on the lock, in order, are the white queen, rook, bishop, and knight. First, we look at the queens:

Then the rooks:

Then the bishops:

And finally the knights:

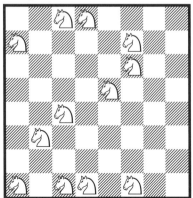

The shapes made by the four sets of pieces are 4, 0, 1, and 2, so the combination is 4012. Unlocking the suitcase reveals two chess knights: a green one and a purple one.

**Page 26: Break It Up, Matey**

We'll ignore the numbers painted on the pieces of the board for now (so we won't include them in the solving diagrams until we reach the end of the puzzle). For convenience, we'll refer to the possible rectangles in which pieces can be placed as A1, A2, A3, A4, B1, B2, B3, and B4, as seen in the diagram above right.

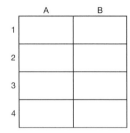

The piece with the black king (piece 4) can't be in A4 or B4, because that would place two pawns on the last row of the board, which is impossible because the pawns would promote when they reached that row. As for the other positions, let's consider what piece can give check to the black king. The king, of course, is not allowed to give check, and the white bishop can't give check because it moves on black squares only, and the black king is on a white square.

The white pawn could check the king by capturing one of the black pawns, if the pieces were aligned as seen at right. However, even if that square were guarded, the black bishop would be able to counter by capturing the pawn—unless the bishop were pinned, which it couldn't be because the rook is the only piece that could pin it, and it's on the same rectangle as the pawn.

The white rook could check the black king in a number of ways. If the rook and king are not in the same column, the rook could move to the left and give check from above (either as shown, or two rows higher). In this case, the king will always be able to escape by moving

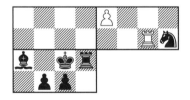

diagonally down to the right, because it's impossible for White to guard that square. The bishop can't guard it because, as noted, it's on the wrong color square. The pawn can't guard it because it's on the same rectangle as the rook. The knight can't guard it because it's on a white square and can only move to a black square from a white square. And the king can't guard it because if it did, it would be in check from a black pawn, as shown.

If the white rook and black king are in the same column, one possibility is the rook moving down the column and capturing a piece to give check. (It must capture a piece to do so because there must be a piece between the rook and the king for the position to be legal; otherwise, the king would already be in check, which is impossible.) In this case, there are multiple ways for Black to avoid mate. The king can escape by moving diagonally (which White still cannot prevent), or the knight can either move between the rook and king to block check (if the rook captures the pawn in the first diagram above) or it can capture the rook (if the rook captures the queen in the second diagram above).

The final possibility, if the rook gives check, is coming from below and moving up the column to capture the pawn (and guarding the square that the king has been escaping to). Even if the king is on the top row of the board, it can respond either by capturing the rook or by moving horizontally to the left, unless white is able to guard both squares. The bishop can't guard both (which would only be possible if the white bishop were in rectangle A1 and the black king were in B4, which we know is impossible), and the king and pawn can't guard either one, so the knight must be guarding at least one. If the white knight is in the rectangle above or below, then the black knight in the same rectangle is positioned to capture the rook in either case. If the white knight is to the right of the king, it can only guard the pawn and not the square to the king's left. The bishop must be guarding that square, but it can't guard it from below, because there isn't room, and if the black king isn't in the top row, it has multiple other escape routes that white cannot block.

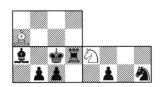 

The white rook could block the three squares above the black king, but it's busy giving check, and while the white king could block those squares, if it were in position to do so, it would be in check by the black bishop, which is impossible.

By elimination then, the white knight is the piece that delivers checkmate. If it gives check from above, then the king cannot be prevented from escaping, for reasons we've already explored (only the pawn can prevent the king escaping diagonally down and only the rook can prevent the king escaping up a row, but the pawn and rook are on the same rectangle), so the white knight must deliver check from below.

The white knight will be immediately captured by a black pawn unless the pawn is pinned, so it must be pinned by the white rook. The white rook can't be in the rectangle immediately below the black king or the black knight in the rook's rectangle will be positioned to capture the white knight, so the rook must be positioned as seen on the far right.

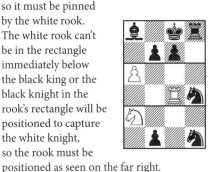 

After the white knight delivers check, it's guarding the king's diagonal escape, so to ensure checkmate, we must guard the square to the king's left, which can now only be accomplished with the white bishop. Now we just have to place the other four pieces in legal positions without blocking the checkmate.

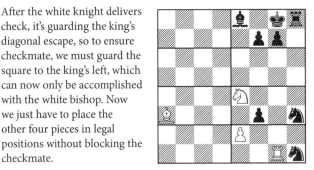

The file between the white rook and black pawn must remain empty for the pawn to be pinned, and only one of the four remaining pieces can be placed in B2 without blocking it, as shown to the right. That leaves three pieces to place in A1, A2, and A4, shown below.

The black queen and white king are in the same column of those rectangles; for the white king not to be in check, the black pawn must be between them, in A2. The white king, then, cannot be in A1 or it would be in check from the black knight in A2, so it's in A4 and the black queen is in A2, giving us this final position (with painted numbers added back to the rectangles). Reading

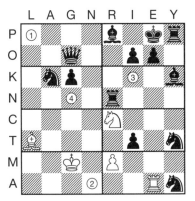

the coordinates of the numbered squares in order (row first, then column), we have (P, L), (A, N), (K, I), (N, G), spelling the combination to the lock, PLANKING. Opening the drawer reveals two chess knights, an orange one and a red one.

**Page 27, top: Knight Game**

We'll ignore the shaded squares for now. This puzzle can mostly be approached like a regular sudoku while keeping in mind the extra squares eliminated by the knight's-move rule, but we'll take a look at some of the trickier steps. Using basic logic, we reach this point, from which there are a couple slightly tricky ways to progress.

|   |   |   |   |   |   |   |   |   |
|---|---|---|---|---|---|---|---|---|
| 3 | 4 |   |   |   | 1 | 2 | 8 |   |
|   |   |   | 3 |   | 2 | 5 | 4 |   |
| 2 |   |   |   |   |   | 3 |   |   |
|   | 3 |   | 1 |   |   |   | 2 |   |
| 4 |   |   |   | 2 |   |   |   | 3 |
|   | 2 |   |   | 3 | 9 |   |   |   |
|   |   | 4 |   |   | 3 |   |   | 2 |
|   | 5 | 3 | 2 |   | 7 |   |   |   |
|   | 6 | 2 | 8 |   |   |   | 3 |   |

Both approaches involve examining the 4's. The two shaded 4's, between them, eliminate all but two squares in the center right box. With that information, there is now only one position for a 4 in the fourth column, in the circled square, placing which opens up many more deductions.

|   |   |   |   |   |   |   |   |   |
|---|---|---|---|---|---|---|---|---|
| 3 | 4 |   |   |   | 1 | 2 | 8 |   |
|   |   |   | 3 |   | 2 | 5 | *4* |   |
| 2 |   |   | ○ |   |   | 3 |   |   |
|   | 3 |   | 1 |   |   |   | 2 |   |
| *4* |   |   |   | 2 |   |   |   | 3 |
|   | 2 |   |   | 3 | 9 | 4 |   | 4 |
|   |   | 4 |   |   | 3 |   |   | 2 |
|   | 5 | 3 | 2 |   | 7 |   |   |   |
|   | 6 | 2 | 8 |   |   |   | 3 |   |

Another options is to look at the third and fourth rows, and the lower middle box; the shaded 4's eliminate the indicated squares in those regions. There cannot be a 4 in the central column of the lower middle box or it would force the 4's in the third and fourth rows to be a knight's move apart, so it must be in the circled square.

|   |   |   |   |   |   |   |   |   |
|---|---|---|---|---|---|---|---|---|
| 3 | *4* |   |   |   | 1 | 2 | 8 |   |
|   |   |   | 3 |   | 2 | 5 | *4* |   |
| 2 |   | 4 | 4 |   |   | 3 |   |   |
|   | 3 |   | 1 | 4 | 4 |   | 2 |   |
| *4* |   |   |   | 2 |   |   |   | 3 |
|   | 2 |   |   | 3 | 9 |   |   |   |
|   |   | *4* |   |   | 3 |   |   | 2 |
|   | 5 | 3 | 2 |   | 7 |   |   |   |
|   | 6 | 2 | 8 | ○ |   |   | 3 |   |

From either of these points, using standard sudoku logic, we can make fairly straightforward progress to this point (a few paired candidates are also indicated). But let's look more closely at what the shaded square can contain. Not 1 (which is a knight's move away); nor 2, 3, 4, 5, or 6 (which are in the same box, row, or column); nor 7 (because that would leave nowhere to place a 7 in the fourth column). It's therefore an 8 or 9; for convenience we'll label it A.

|   |   |   |   |   |   |   |   |   |
|---|---|---|---|---|---|---|---|---|
| 3 | 4 | 5 | 9 |   | 1 | 2 | 8 |   |
|   |   |   | 3 |   | 2 | 5 | 4 |   |
| 2 |   |   | 4 |   | 5 | 3 |   |   |
| 5 | 3 |   | 1 | 4 | (68) |   | 2 |   |
| 4 |   |   | 57 | 2 | (68) |   |   | 3 |
|   | 2 |   | 57 | 3 | 9 |   |   |   |
|   |   | 4 | 6 | 59 | 3 |   |   | 2 |
|   | 5 | 3 | 2 | 1 | 7 |   |   |   |
|   | 6 | 2 | 8 | 59 | 4 |   | 3 |   |

That A eliminates two cells in the box below, creating a pair in the left-hand column. That's enough information to eliminate all but one cell for the A in the upper left. That A eliminates the entire central column in the upper center box, so A can't be an 8 (which must be among those cells) and therefore A is 9.

|   |   |   |   |   |   |   |   |   |
|---|---|---|---|---|---|---|---|---|
| 3 | 4 | 5 | 9 |   | 1 | 2 | 8 |   |
|   |   | A | 3 |   | 2 | 5 | 4 |   |
| 2 |   |   | 4 |   | 5 | 3 |   |   |
| 5 | 3 |   | 1 | 4 | (68) |   | 2 |   |
| 4 | A |   | 57 | 2 | (68) |   |   | 3 |
|   | 2 |   | 57 | 3 | 9 |   |   |   |
|   |   | 4 | 6 | 59 | 3 |   |   | 2 |
| A | 5 | 3 | 2 | 1 | 7 |   |   |   |
| A | 6 | 2 | 8 | 59 | 4 |   | 3 |   |

**72**

---

From this point, straightforward sudoku logic (plus anti-knight eliminations, of course) will get us nearly all the way to the end, to the point shown here, with all possible candidates filled in for the unknown squares. To proceed from here, let's label the three squares in the upper middle box as A, B, and C.

|   |   |   |   |   |   |   |   |   |
|---|---|---|---|---|---|---|---|---|
| 3 | 4 | 5 | 9 | 67 | 1 | 2 | 8 | 67 |
| 678 | 1 | 9 | 3 | 678 | 2 | 5 | 4 | 67 |
| 2 | 78 | 68 | 4 | 678 | 5 | 3 | 9 | 1 |
| 5 | 3 | 7 | 1 | 4 | 68 | 68 | 2 | 9 |
| 4 | 9 | 1 | 7 | 2 | 68 | 68 | 5 | 3 |
| 68 | 2 | 68 | 5 | 3 | 9 | 1 | 7 | 4 |
| 78 | 78 | 4 | 6 | 5 | 3 | 9 | 1 | 2 |
| 9 | 5 | 3 | 2 | 1 | 7 | 4 | 6 | 8 |
| 1 | 6 | 2 | 8 | 9 | 4 | 7 | 3 | 5 |

The B eliminates all but one cell from the box to its left (which further narrows down its candidates to 7 and 8); that, in turn, pins down the B's position in the lower left box.

|   |   |   |   |   |   |   |   |   |
|---|---|---|---|---|---|---|---|---|
| 3 | 4 | 5 | 9 | 67/A | 1 | 2 | 8 | 67 |
| 678 | 1 | 9 | 3 | 678/B | 2 | 5 | 4 | 67 |
| 2 | 78/B | 68 | 4 | 678/C | 5 | 3 | 9 | 1 |
| 5 | 3 | 7 | 1 | 4 | 68 | 68 | 2 | 9 |
| 4 | 9 | 1 | 7 | 2 | 68 | 68 | 5 | 3 |
| 68 | 2 | 68 | 5 | 3 | 9 | 1 | 7 | 4 |
| 78/B | 78 | 4 | 6 | 5 | 3 | 9 | 1 | 2 |
| 9 | 5 | 3 | 2 | 1 | 7 | 4 | 6 | 8 |
| 1 | 6 | 2 | 8 | 9 | 4 | 7 | 3 | 5 |

The C's position eliminates two of its three possible locations in both the upper left box and the center box (the latter of which narrows down its candidates to 6 and 8). Placing C's in those two squares, in turn, allows us to place two more C's.

|   |   |   |   |   |   |   |   |   |
|---|---|---|---|---|---|---|---|---|
| 3 | 4 | 5 | 9 | 67/A | 1 | 2 | 8 | 67 |
| 678/C | 1 | 9 | 3 | 78/B | 2 | 5 | 4 | 67 |
| 2 | 78/B | 68 | 4 | 678/C | 5 | 3 | 9 | 1 |
| 5 | 3 | 7 | 1 | 4 | 68/C | 68 | 2 | 9 |
| 4 | 9 | 1 | 7 | 2 | 68 | 68/C | 5 | 3 |
| 68 | 2 | 68/C | 5 | 3 | 9 | 1 | 7 | 4 |
| 78/B | 78 | 4 | 6 | 5 | 3 | 9 | 1 | 2 |
| 9 | 5 | 3 | 2 | 1 | 7 | 4 | 6 | 8 |
| 1 | 6 | 2 | 8 | 9 | 4 | 7 | 3 | 5 |

Now we're able to jump-start the last steps in either of two ways. In the upper left, with C's candidates narrowed down, the pair of 6/8 squares means that B can only be 7. Alternately, in the center left box, the shaded square can't be either B or C, so it can only be A. But we know A isn't 8, so A must be 6.

|   |   |   |   |   |   |   |   |   |
|---|---|---|---|---|---|---|---|---|
| 3 | 4 | 5 | 9 | 67/A | 1 | 2 | 8 | 67 |
| 68/C | 1 | 9 | 3 | 78/B | 2 | 5 | 4 | 67 |
| 2 | 78/B | 68 | 4 | 68/C | 5 | 3 | 9 | 1 |
| 5 | 3 | 7 | 1 | 4 | 68/C | 68 | 2 | 9 |
| 4 | 9 | 1 | 7 | 2 | 68 | 68/C | 5 | 3 |
| 68 | 2 | 68/C | 5 | 3 | 9 | 1 | 7 | 4 |
| 78/B | 78 | 4 | 6 | 5 | 3 | 9 | 1 | 2 |
| 9 | 5 | 3 | 2 | 1 | 7 | 4 | 6 | 8 |
| 1 | 6 | 2 | 8 | 9 | 4 | 7 | 3 | 5 |

Either of these observations allows us to quickly fill in the rest of the grid, which looks like this (with its shaded squares restored). The logo on the lock tells us the order in which to read the numbers in the shaded squares, giving us the combination: 897795112. Opening the safe reveals two chess knights, a blue one and a yellow one.

|   |   |   |   |   |   |   |   |   |
|---|---|---|---|---|---|---|---|---|
| 3 | 4 | 5 | 9 | 6 | 1 | 2 | 8 | 7 |
| 8 | 1 | 9 | 3 | 7 | 2 | 5 | 4 | 6 |
| 2 | 7 | 6 | 4 | 8 | 5 | 3 | 9 | 1 |
| 5 | 3 | 7 | 1 | 4 | 8 | 6 | 2 | 9 |
| 4 | 9 | 1 | 7 | 2 | 6 | 8 | 5 | 3 |
| 6 | 2 | 8 | 5 | 3 | 9 | 1 | 7 | 4 |
| 7 | 8 | 4 | 6 | 5 | 3 | 9 | 1 | 2 |
| 9 | 5 | 3 | 2 | 1 | 7 | 4 | 6 | 8 |
| 1 | 6 | 2 | 8 | 9 | 4 | 7 | 3 | 5 |

**Page 27, bottom: I Was Told There'd Be No Algebra**

The clues on the right, when answered correctly, give the following five-letter words: NAPES, BATHE, BAUER, NAUGA, PECHE, QATAR, RECAP, and KESHA. Kamala noticed that the letter patterns of the answers matched the letters in the chess notation, which is not actually chess notation at all. For instance, if we replace the 4 and 6 in "Qa4–a6" with T and R, it spells QATAR. Matching up the answers with the eight "chess moves," and setting off the replaced letters with parentheses for easier reference, we get:

Qa4–a6 = QA(T)A(R)
Re1–a3 = RE(C)A(P)
Na3–e8 = NA(P)E(S)
Ba4–h7 = BA(T)H(E)
Pe1–h7 = PE(C)H(E)
Ke8–h2 = KE(S)H(A)
Na5–g2 = NA(U)G(A)
Ba5–e6 = BA(U)E(R)

Examining the above, we see that each number is always replaced by the same letter. For instance, C corresponds to 1, A to 2, and so on. Reading the letters in order from 1 to 8 spells the password, CAPTURES. Opening the suitcase reveals two chess knights, a gold one and a silver one.


**Page 28: Weighted Pieces**

For convenience, we will refer to the pieces by their chess abbreviations (P = pawn, N = knight, B = bishop, R = rook, Q = queen, and K = king), and we'll use capital letters for white pieces, lowercase letters for black pieces. To start with, let's examine the three scales with these weighings: P+Q+n+q=K, n+q=Q, and 2P+K<3Q. The maximum any piece can weigh is 12, and the minimum sum of four different pieces is 10 (1+2+3+4), so K is either 10, 11, or 12. The four weights on the left must be, in some order, 1+2+3+4, 1+2+3+5, 1+2+4+5, or 1+2+3+6. Let's look at the possibilities for n+q=Q for each. (Whichever weight is unused will be the white pawn.)

1+2+3+4=10: 1+2=3 (P=4), 1+3=4 (P=2)
1+2+3+5=11: 1+2=3 (P=5), 2+3=5 (P=1)
1+2+4+5=12: 1+4=5 (P=2)
1+2+3+6=12: 1+2=3 (P=6)

In the cases where Q=3, 3Q is always less than K, so we can eliminate those options. Let's calculate 2P+K and 3Q for the other three options:

K=10, P=2, Q=4: 2P+K=14, 3Q=12, 2P+K>3Q
K=11, P=1, Q=5: 2P+K=13, 3Q=15, 2P+K<3Q
K=12, P=2, Q=5: 2P+K=16, 3Q=15, 2P+K>3Q.

Only the second set of values works, so P=1, Q=5, K=11, and the black knight and queen are 2 and 3 in some order. Now let's look at the scales with these weighings: N+p=R and N<p. The sum N+p=R uses three values that haven't yet been assigned; the remaining weights are 4, 6, 7, 8, 9, 10, and 12. The minimum possible total is 4+6=10, which is the only way to make a sum of 10. The only available number higher than 10 is 12, for which there is only one way to make a sum: 4+8=12. These, then, are the only two possibilities for this weighing, so the white rook weighs 10 or 12, and in either case the 4 must be included on the other side of the scale. Since N<p, N=4 and the black pawn weighs either 6 or 8.

Let's now look at the scale with the weighing B+Q=2k. Q=5, so B+5=2k, which means B must be an odd number. The only odd numbers available are 7 and 9, so the black king weighs either 6 or 7 (7+5=2×6, 9+5=2×7).

Finally, we look at the last remaining scale: N+B+q+k=2b+r. N=4, B+k=13 (7+6) or 16 (9+7), and q=2 or 3. The 10 and 12 weights remain unassigned; the white rook accounts for one of them, but the other must be either the black bishop or black rook. Let's look at all the possible combinations for N+(B+k)+q: 4+13+2=19, 4+13+3=20, 4+16+2=22, or 4+16+3=23. The black bishop can't be the piece that weighs 10 or 12, because if it weighs at least 10, 2b+r will weigh at least 26 (since every weight lower than 6 is already accounted for). The black rook weighs 10 or 12, then. This means that 2b+r must be an even number, so we can eliminate two of the four combinations, leaving us with either 4+13+3=20 or 4+16+2=22. The former is impossible, because for 2b+r to equal 20, the black bishop would have to weigh 4 or 5, and both of those weights have already been assigned. So the remaining total is the correct one (and B=9, k=7, q=2, and by elimination n=3): 2b+r=22. The only values that work are b=6 and r=10, so by elimination R=12 and p=8. The correct weights for all pieces are shown at right.

We can now calculate the combination. 1+8+4+3=16, 9+6+12+10=37, and 5+2+11+7=25. The combination is 16-37-25. Opening the safe reveals two chess knights, a pink one and a gray one.


**Page 29: Words of Wisdom**

Firstly, if your password is longer than 7 letters, it is not correct, but if it is a three-word phrase, you're on the right track.

The 16 names in all caps in the first paragraph of the article are all hidden, one per sentence, in the story—but each name has an extra letter in it. For instance, in the first sentence, SPASSKY is hidden in "room'S PASS KEY," with an extra E inserted. By paragraph, all the hidden names are:

SPASSKY + E (room'S PASS KEY)
FISCHER + N (mufFINS CHERry)
STEINITZ + D (faSTED IN IT Zero)
LOPEZ + L (LOL PEZ)
POLGAR + E (tadPOLE GARnished)
CARUANA + S (iCARUS AN Arrogant)
LASKER + S (fLASK SERenely)

EUWE + N (werE UNWEll)
ANAND + A (bANANA Daiquiri)
ARONIAN + P (macARONI PANcakes)

LARSEN + M (aLARM SENsibly)
SHORT + A (thankS HORATio)
MENCHIK + S (MENSCH, I Know)
SHIROV + T (SHIRT OVer)
KARPOV + E (kinfolK ARE POVerty-stricken)
ADAMS + R (stellAR DAMSel)

73

The added letters, in order, spell ENDLESS NAP MASTER, which is certainly what Queenie seems to be. This, however, is too long to be the password. What we need to do is take it literally: if we make NAP and MASTER endless by deleting their last letters, we are left with NA and MASTE. Combining those gives us the password: NAMASTE. Typing that password into the computer causes the monitor itself to pop open, rather unexpectedly, revealing two chess knights inside, a white one and a black one.

### Pages 30–31: Knights of the Round Table

The youngest knight was no younger than 21, and the oldest knight was no older than 89. (clue 2)

No two age differences of adjacent knights were the same (clue 3), so the minimum age difference of the youngest and oldest knights is 1+2+3+4+5+6+7+8+9+10+11=66. Therefore, if the youngest knight is 21, the oldest is at least 87; similarly, if the oldest knight is 89, the youngest is at most 23. So the youngest knight is 21, 22, or 23, and the oldest is 87, 88, or 89.

Within that age range, the Red, Black, and Yellow Knights could be 21, 42, and 84; or 22, 44, and 88, respectively (clue 11). But the Black Knight cannot be 42, because the knight who is 42 is four seats away from the Pink Knight (clue 7) and the Black Knight is within three seats of the Pink Knight (clue 16). Therefore the Red Knight is 22, the Black Knight is 44, and the Yellow Knight is 88. The Black Knight must be seated next to the knight who is 42 (since the age difference of 2 cannot be subdivided), so the Pink Knight is seated three seats counterclockwise from the Black Knight, and Sir Hector is four seats counterclockwise from the Pink Knight. The age range from youngest to oldest can now be 21–88, 22–88, or 22–89. (It cannot be 21–89, because we know there are knights aged 22 and 88, and if all four ages were represented, 21 & 22 and 88 & 89 would both have age differences of 1 year, which contradicts clue 3.)

Of the three knights not in the clue 12 triads (Sir Ironside, the Gray Knight, and the Orange Knight), two are the oldest and youngest. The Gray and Orange Knights can't be the two that are the oldest and youngest, since it is at least the case that either the Red Knight is the youngest or the Yellow Knight is the oldest. Therefore Sir Ironside must be either youngest or oldest, and the knights on either side of him must have complementary-colored nicknames. The Gray Knight can't be the other of the three who is the oldest or youngest, then, since gray has no complementary color, so the Orange Knight is either youngest or oldest (and Sir Ironside is either the Red Knight or the Yellow Knight). If Sir Ironside were the youngest (at age 22), he would be the Red Knight, the Orange Knight would be the oldest (at age 89), the Yellow next oldest (at age 88). With the Orange Knight seated to Sir Ironside's left, the Blue Knight would have to be to his right (clue 10). This leaves only one possible way for two complementary colors to be adjacent: if the Purple Knight is seated to the left of the Yellow Knight. That seat is two seats away from the oldest knight, and Sir Dinas must be in the corresponding seat on the opposite side of the oldest knight (clue 9), but since the Blue Knight has already been placed there, this is impossible, since Sir Dinas is not the Blue Knight (clue 4).

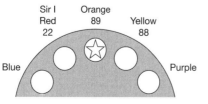

Sir Ironside, therefore, is the Yellow Knight and is the oldest (at age 88), the Orange Knight is the youngest (at age 21), and the Red Knight is the next youngest (at age 22). The Blue Knight must be seated to Sir Ironside's left (clue 10), which places Sir Clarence directly opposite (at 7:00, per clue 4); now the only way for adjacent knights to be complementary is for the Green Knight to be seated to the right of the Red Knight.

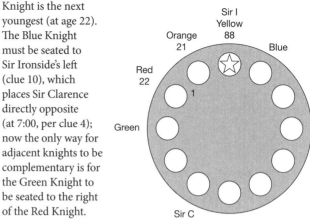

We now know that the age differences are the numbers 1–10 and 12, since the difference between the youngest and oldest is 67, which can only be made up of 1+2+3+4+5+6+7+8+9+10+12. The possible pairs of age differences for which one is twice the other are 1 & 2, 2 & 4, 3 & 6, 4 & 8, 5 & 10, and 6 & 12. We can eliminate 1 & 2, however, since the two knights aged 21 & 22 are 1 year apart and the two knights aged 42 & 44 are two years apart, so those differences do not appear sequentially. None of the triads overlap, so 2 & 4 and 4 & 8 cannot both be represented, since they both contain 4, nor can 3 & 6 and 6 & 12, since they both contain 6. Therefore 5 & 10 must be one of the pairs. Sir Edward is 5 years older than the Gold Knight, and so Sir Edward must be either the Pink or Silver Knight (not the Green Knight, who has the Red Knight seated to his left and not the Gold Knight), and he is 10 years younger than the knight to his right.

The oldest and youngest knights are not part of any of the three triads in clue 12; the only other knight *not* involved is the Gray Knight, so the Blue, Red, and Green Knights are in triads. One set, then, must be the knights at 1:00, 2:00, and 3:00, and another set must be the knights at 8:00, 9:00, and 10:00. The Gray Knight, then, is at either 4:00 or 7:00 and the other "central" knight (Pink or Silver) is at 5:00 or 6:00.

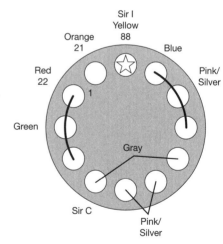

The 42-year old knight is four seats away from the Pink Knight, who is seated either at 2:00, 5:00, or 6:00; this means the 42-year-old knight can only be at 6:00. Why? All the other seats have an unbridgeable age gap. For instance, if the Pink Knight is at 5:00 and the 42-year-old at 9:00, that creates a 20-year age gap with the Red Knight. A quick examination of the other possibilities will similarly rule them out. With the 42-year-old knight placed at 6:00, we can also place the Black Knight at 5:00, the Pink Knight at 2:00, Sir Hector at 10:00, and identify the 42-year-old knight as the Silver Knight. The Silver Knight is at the center of the last triad from clue 12, so the Gray Knight must be at 4:00, and Sir Agrivaine is three seats away (clue 13), but not clockwise from the Gray Knight (where Sir Clarence is seated), so Sir Agrivaine is the Blue Knight, at 1:00. The only option for the age gap between the Silver Knight and Sir Clarence, per clue 12, is 4 years, so Sir Clarence is 38 years old.

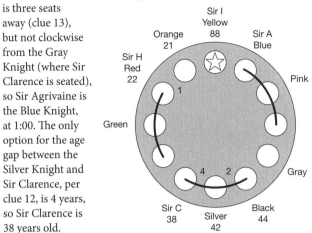

Sir Edward, 5 years older than his left-hand neighbor, can't be the Silver Knight, so he's the Pink Knight, and the Gold Knight is at 3:00. By elimination the White and Purple Knights are at 7:00 and 8:00 in some order, so Sir Dinas is at 4:00 or 5:00, but he's not the Black Knight (who's 2 years older than the knight to his left, contradicting clue 17), so he's the Gray Knight and is 53 years old, and the Purple Knight is at 8:00; by elimination the White Knight is at 7:00 and is Sir Clarence. The set of four knights in clue 6 must be somewhere in the range of 5:00 to 9:00; in any case the Silver Knight is included, but since Lionel isn't the Silver Knight (clue 14), Sir Bryan is. The Green Knight's age differences with his neighbors can be 3 & 6 years or 6 & 12 years, but the person to his right must be younger than 38, and $22 + 6 + 12 = 40$, so the differences are 3 & 6 in some order and the knight to Clarence's left is $22 + 3 + 6 = 31$, 7 years younger than Clarence, and the Green Knight is either 25 or 28 years old.

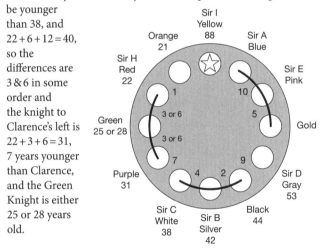

The age differences between 3:00 & 4:00, and between 12:00 and 1:00 are 8 and 12 in some combination, so the ages of the knights to the right of Sir Dinas are either 61, 66, 76, and 88; or 65, 70, 80, and 88. The only possible combination for clue 8 is if Sir Fergus is the Black Knight (age 44) and Sir Kay is the Gold Knight (and is age 65). Sir Lionel, then, can only be the Green Knight (clue 6). Geraint is older than Jerome, so Geraint is the Purple Knight and Jerome is the Orange Knight. The ages all around the table, then, are 21, 22, 25 or 28, 31, 38, 42, 44, 53, 65, 70, 80, and 88. Not counting the Green Knight, three of the ages are divisible by 7 (21, 42, and 70), and three are divisible by 5 (65, 70, and 80). For there to be more ages divisible by 7 than by 5, the Green Knight must be 28 years old. In summary:

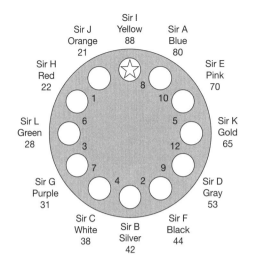

Sir Ironside, the Yellow Knight, is 88 years old.
Sir Agrivaine, the Blue Knight, is 80 years old.
Sir Edward, the Pink Knight, is 70 years old.
Sir Kay, the Gold Knight, is 65 years old.
Sir Dinas, the Gray Knight, is 53 years old.
Sir Fergus, the Black Knight, is 44 years old.
Sir Bryan, the Silver Knight, is 42 years old.
Sir Clarence, the White Knight, is 38 years old.
Sir Geraint, the Purple Knight, is 31 years old.
Sir Lionel, the Green Knight, is 28 years old.
Sir Hector, the Red Knight, is 22 years old.
Sir Jerome, the Orange Knight, is 21 years old.

**Pages 32–33: Escape Plans**

First, we can start by blocking out any time slots that are explicitly given in the clues. Bette & Frieda were not available from 4:30 on (clue 2); Ahmad and Heath were not available before 3:30 (clue 5); Ciara was not available between 2:00 and 4:00 but was available from 4:00 to 4:30 (clue 7); Ewan was unavailable from 1:00 to 4:00 (clue 8).

There are 15 half-hour segments of the schedule, and Greg's pattern of available and unavailable times (clue 4) must take up at least $3 + 2 + 3 + 2 + 3 = 13$ of them. This means that, because of the way the possible arrangements overlap, he must have been available in the half hours 1:00–1:30, 3:30–4:00, and 6:00–6:30, and we can add 6:00–6:30 to the times that Ewan was not available, since Greg and Ewan were never available at the same time.

Ewan, per clue 3, was available for exactly 90 minutes. That time must have been consecutive (as must also be the case for Ahmad and Ichiko), because only one person had a lone half-hour time slot (clue 6), and that person also had the longest available time slot, which was necessarily longer than an hour. We can therefore eliminate 12:00–1:00 and 6:30–7:30 from Ewan's schedule, leaving a window from 4:00–6:00, within which his 90-minute block must include 4:30–5:30. Per clue 4, Greg was unavailable from 4:30 to 5:30. Eliminating those times forces Greg's availability to include 3:00–3:30 and 6:30–7:00. Our solving grid now looks like the one on the next page.

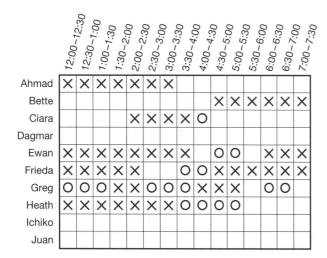

| | 12:00–12:30 | 12:30–1:00 | 1:00–1:30 | 1:30–2:00 | 2:00–2:30 | 2:30–3:00 | 3:00–3:30 | 3:30–4:00 | 4:00–4:30 | 4:30–5:00 | 5:00–5:30 | 5:30–6:00 | 6:00–6:30 | 6:30–7:00 | 7:00–7:30 |
|---|---|---|---|---|---|---|---|---|---|---|---|---|---|---|---|
| Ahmad | X | X | X | X | X | X | X | | | | | | | | |
| Bette | | | | | | | | | | | X | X | X | X | X |
| Ciara | | | | | X | X | X | X | O | | | | | | |
| Dagmar | | | | | | | | | | | | | | | |
| Ewan | X | X | X | X | X | X | X | X | | O | O | | X | X | X |
| Frieda | | | | | | | | | | X | X | X | X | X | |
| Greg | | | O | | | O | O | | X | X | | | O | O | |
| Heath | X | X | X | X | X | X | X | | | | | | | | |
| Ichiko | | | | | | | | | | | | | | | |
| Juan | | | | | | | | | | | | | | | |

Heath and Frieda's schedules overlapped by an hour (clue 9) and that hour can only be 3:30–4:30. Since Heath was available for twice as long as Frieda (and because his availability was uninterrupted), he must have also been available from 4:30 to 5:30. Also, since his availability is at most four hours, Frieda was available for two hours at most, and we can eliminate everything before 2:30 from her schedule. Greg's schedule cannot include 4:00–4:30, or he would share the same consecutive hour with both Frieda and Heath, which contradicts clue 9. He was therefore available from 2:30–3:00, unavailable for an hour before that, and available for 90 minutes before that.

For Frieda's schedule to overlap Greg's by exactly one hour (clue 9), she must have been available 3:00–3:30 but not 2:30–3:00. Since she was available for 90 minutes, Heath was available for twice that: three hours, until 6:30. For his schedule to overlap Greg's by an hour, Greg must have been available 5:30–6:00 (and not 7:00–7:30). Ewan therefore wasn't available then (clue 4), and his other available half hour was 4:00–4:30.

Now consider clue 10. There are 15 half-hour time slots, and the five time slots mentioned (Juan, Ichiko, Bette, Ciara, and Dagmar, in that order) were all different lengths, so they were 1, 2, 3, 4, and 5 half-hour segments long, in some order. Bette wasn't available after 4:30, so Ciara and Dagmar accounted for all of that between them, as well as Ciara's 4:00–4:30 block—7 half hours in total. The 7 segments could be comprised of 2+5 or 3+4, but Ichiko must have had the 90-minute segment (clue 3), so Ciara and Dagmar's blocks were 1 hour and 2.5 hours, in some order. By elimination,

Juan and Bette's slots were a half hour and 2 hours, in some order. The five segments didn't overlap, so Bette was unavailable from 4:00 to 4:30, and Ichiko's only 90-minute window was between Juan and Bette's blocks, so we can eliminate 12:00–12:30 and all times from 3:30 on for Ichiko. Based on the minimum length of everyone's blocks, we can add some availability at the beginnings and ends of the known blocks, as shown here.

| | 12:00–12:30 | 12:30–1:00 | 1:00–1:30 | 1:30–2:00 | 2:00–2:30 | 2:30–3:00 | 3:00–3:30 | 3:30–4:00 | 4:00–4:30 | 4:30–5:00 | 5:00–5:30 | 5:30–6:00 | 6:00–6:30 | 6:30–7:00 | 7:00–7:30 |
|---|---|---|---|---|---|---|---|---|---|---|---|---|---|---|---|
| Ahmad | X | X | X | X | X | X | X | | | | | | | | |
| Bette | | | | | | | | O | X | X | X | X | X | X | X |
| Ciara | | | | X | X | X | X | O | O | | | | | | |
| Dagmar | | | | | | | | | | | | | O | O | |
| Ewan | X | X | X | X | X | X | X | X | O | O | O | X | X | X | X |
| Frieda | X | X | X | X | X | O | O | O | O | X | X | X | X | X | X |
| Greg | O | O | O | X | X | O | O | O | X | X | X | O | O | O | X |
| Heath | X | X | X | X | X | O | O | O | O | O | O | O | X | X | X |
| Ichiko | X | | | | | | | X | X | X | X | X | X | X | X |
| Juan | O | | | | | | | | | | | | | | |

Ahmad wasn't available any time that Ewan was (clue 1), so we can eliminate 4:00–5:30, as well as 3:30–4:00, which is too short to fit his 90-minute block of availability; of the two remaining hours, he must have been available from 6:00 to 7:00.

Whichever of Bette or Juan had the half-hour slot in clue 10, they must also have had the longest time slot (clue 6). Bette can, at most, have fit in a 3-hour slot from 12:00 to 3:00, which is as long as Heath's time slot, so she can't be the one person with the longest time slot. Juan had the half-hour slot, ending at 12:30; Ichiko's 90-minute slot ran from 12:30 to 2:00, and Bette's 2-hour slot was 2:00–4:00. With those availabilities marked, there are now only three half-hour blocks in which there aren't at least two people available (1:30–2:00, 2:00–2:30, 7:00–7:30), and the only two that are consecutive are 1:30–2:00 and 2:00–2:30, so Ichiko and Bette are the only people available in each of those slots, respectively.

| | 12:00–12:30 | 12:30–1:00 | 1:00–1:30 | 1:30–2:00 | 2:00–2:30 | 2:30–3:00 | 3:00–3:30 | 3:30–4:00 | 4:00–4:30 | 4:30–5:00 | 5:00–5:30 | 5:30–6:00 | 6:00–6:30 | 6:30–7:00 | 7:00–7:30 |
|---|---|---|---|---|---|---|---|---|---|---|---|---|---|---|---|
| Ahmad | X | X | X | X | X | X | X | X | X | X | X | | O | O | |
| Bette | | | | X | O | O | O | O | X | X | X | X | X | X | X |
| Ciara | | | | X | X | X | X | O | O | | | | | | |
| Dagmar | | | | X | X | | | | | | | | O | O | |
| Ewan | X | X | X | X | X | X | X | X | O | O | O | X | X | X | X |
| Frieda | X | X | X | X | X | O | O | O | X | X | X | X | X | X | X |
| Greg | O | O | O | X | X | O | O | O | X | O | O | X | O | O | X |
| Heath | X | X | X | X | X | X | O | O | O | O | O | O | X | X | X |
| Ichiko | X | O | O | O | X | X | X | X | X | X | X | X | X | X | X |
| Juan | O | X | | X | X | | | | | | | | | | |

No one but Ciara can fulfill the description in clue 12; Dagmar cannot because she has more availability than Juan (clue 13), who has more than 3 hours available (clue 6), and everyone else has obvious contradictions. Ciara, then, is unavailable 5:00–5:30, and Dagmar completes the clue 10 set with a block of availability from

5:00 to 7:30 (and no availability 4:30–5:00). Juan didn't have more than one single half-hour slot, so he was unavailable 1:00–1:30. His long stretch of availability must be longer than Heath's three hours and so is at least 7 half-hour segments long; accordingly, it must include 4:00–6:00. That brings us here:

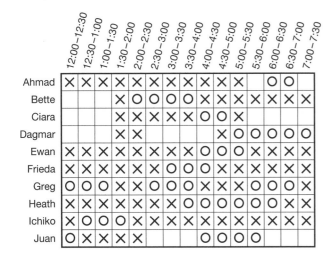

Now: where can there be a one-hour block in which six people are available? The first slots that can fit six people at all are 3:30–4:00 and 4:00–4:30, but the same six people are not potentially available in both. The only other such window is 5:30–6:30, so Ahmad, Ciara, and Juan must all be available for that full hour (and Ahmad is unavailable 7:00–7:30 per clue 3, while Ciara is unavailable 6:30–7:30 per clue 12). Since 1:30–2:30 represent the only times when a single person was available for a time slot, someone else besides Dagmar must have been available 7:00–7:30, and by elimination that can only be Juan. There were no other single half-hour slots (clue 6), so he was also available 6:30–7:00.

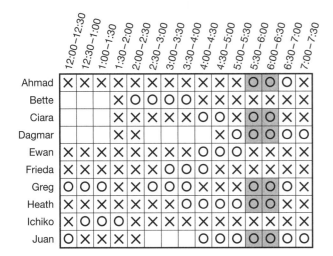

There were also two one-hour slots in which five people were available (clue 15). One must be 12:30–1:30 (five people can be available 12:00–12:30, but one is Juan, who isn't available 12:30–1:00), and the other can only be 3:00–4:00 (only four people can be available 2:30–3:00, and only four people can be available in both slots from 3:30 to 4:30). Bette, Ciara, and Dagmar are therefore available for the full hour from 12:30 to 1:30; and Dagmar and Juan are available for the full hour from 3:00 to 4:00, giving us the grid at the top of the next column.

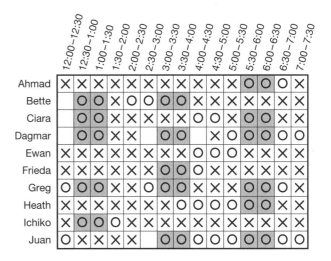

All of Ciara's time slots were an hour (clue 12), so she was unavailable 12:00–12:30. None of Bette's time slots were an hour (clue 14), so she was available 12:00–12:30. Juan is currently available for 5 hours in total. If Dagmar were available in every slot that isn't currently accounted for, that would total 6 hours—and per clue 13, that must be the case, so Dagmar was available for every remaining one of her time slots, and Juan was unavailable 2:30–3:30. We can now see the full schedule:

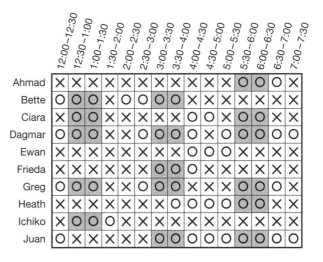

In summary, Ahmad, Ciara, Dagmar, Greg, Heath, and Juan went to The Great Escapes from 5:30 to 6:30.

**Page 34: Evolving Doors, The First Room**

If Door 1 were the correct door and a truth-teller, then Door 2 would lie and say Door 1 was not the correct door, and Door 1 would truthfully report Door 1's statement, so this possibility can be eliminated. If Door 1 were the correct door and a liar, then Door 2 would truthfully say Door 1 was the correct door, and Door 1 would lie and say the opposite, so this can also be eliminated, and Door 2 must be the correct door.

Let's just confirm the other options: If Door 1 were the wrong door and a truth-letter, Door 2 would lie and tell you Door 1 was the correct door and Door 1 would accurately report that. If Door 1 were the wrong door and a liar, then Door 2 would truthfully say that Door 1 was the wrong door, and Door 1 would say the opposite.

We therefore know that Door 2 is the correct door, but we do not know which door is telling the truth. Let's look at Door 2's first statement. Any door, whether a liar or truth-teller, would say that it was the correct door to exit the room, so this is a true statement. Door 1, then, is the liar and Door 2 is the truth-teller.

Per Door 2's true statement, the passcode consists of ascending odd numbers, but it doesn't contain a 7 (since Door 1, lying, said that it did), so the passcode is 1359, entered into Door 2's keypad.

**Page 35: Evolving Doors, The Second Room**

Let's examine Door 1's first statement and Door 3's first statement. For the six possible arrangments of truth-teller, liar, and alternator, we get these truth values for all statements:

| Door 1:<br>Truth-teller | Door 2:<br>Liar | Door 3:<br>Alternator |
| --- | --- | --- |
| T | F | T |
| T | F | F |
| T | F | T |

| Door 1:<br>Truth-teller | Door 2:<br>Alternator | Door 3:<br>Liar |
| --- | --- | --- |
| T | T | F |
| T | F | F |
| T | T | F |

| Door 1:<br>Liar | Door 2:<br>Truth-teller | Door 3:<br>Alternator |
| --- | --- | --- |
| F | T | F |
| F | T | T |
| F | T | F |

| Door 1:<br>Liar | Door 2:<br>Alternator | Door 3:<br>Truth-teller |
| --- | --- | --- |
| F | F | T |
| F | T | T |
| F | F | T |

| Door 1:<br>Alternator | Door 2:<br>Truth-teller | Door 3:<br>Liar |
| --- | --- | --- |
| F | T | F |
| T | T | F |
| F | T | F |

| Door 1:<br>Alternator | Door 2:<br>Liar | Door 3:<br>Truth-teller |
| --- | --- | --- |
| T | F | T |
| F | F | T |
| T | F | T |

Door 2's first statement can only be made in the second and fourth of these possibilities (that is, when Door 1 and Door 2's first statements are either both true or both false). In either case, Door 2 is the alternator and thus Door 2's second statement is true, which is only the case for the latter of those two options. Therefore Door 1 is the liar, Door 2 is the alternator (and starts with a false statement), and Door 3 is the truth-teller.

All of Door 3's statements are true, so the password contains at least two letters from SLOW and at least two from CHAP (in those positions). Since each word's letters are completely distinct, the password must contain exactly two letters from each word. The words that fit those criteria are: SLAP, SHOP, SHAW, CLOP, CLAW, and CHOW. Since Door 1 is a liar, the password contains at most one letter in the word CHAW. That eliminates SHAW, CLAW, and CHOW, leaving SLAP, SHOP, and CLOP. Door 2's third statement is a lie, so the password contains at most one of the letters in the word CLAP, which eliminates SLAP and CLOP; the password is SHOP. Since Door 1's third statement is false, and only Door 3's third statement is true, Door 3 is the correct door in which to enter the password.

**Page 36: Evolving Doors, The Third Room**

Each of Door 4's statements indicates a pair of letters that the password may or may not include, depending on which statements are true. These are, in order, RT ("retweet," for short), PO (brief version of "post office"), NO (word between "spare" and "expense"), GO (opposite Free Parking on a Monopoly board), UG (center of [Victor] Hugo), ST (beginning or ending of [Ziggy] Stardust), WA (state that borders OR and ID), and AL (Gore, Green, Roker, or Unser).

Of the first statements of Doors 1, 2, and 3, only one can be true; if more than one is true, there will always be multiple statements among Door 4's statements that must be both true and false. (For instance, Door 4's first statement begins with a consonant and doesn't contain the letter A, which would cause a contradiction if both Door 2 and Door 3's first statements were true.)

If Door 1's first statement is true, then Door 4's true statements are the first, sixth, seventh, and eighth, which indicate that the password includes RT, ST, WA, and AL. These four letter pairs can be rearranged to spell STALWART, a word meaning "loyal." But if Door 1 is the truth-teller, the password is a country, so Door 1 is not the truth-teller.

If Door 2's first statement is true, then Door 4's true statements are the second, fourth, sixth, and eighth, which indicate that the password includes PO, GO, ST, and AL. These four letter pairs can be rearranged to spell GOALPOST, something seen on a sports field. This is in line with Door 2's final statement, so Door 2 could be the truth-teller.

If Door 3's first statement is true, then Door 4's true statements are the first, second, fifth, and eighth, which indicate that the password includes RT, PO, UG, and AL. These four letter pairs can be rearranged to spell PORTUGAL, a country. But Door 3's second statement asserts that the password is a word meaning "loyal," so Door 3 is also not the truth-teller, confirming that Door 2 is the truth-teller and GOALPOST is the password.

(One of the clues is false in all cases; appropriately, it's the one that indicates the letters NO.)

Both of Door 3's statements are false, so Door 3 is the liar and Door 1 is the alternator, which means Door 1's second statement is true. Door 2 is the truth-teller, so naturally Door 2's second statement is also true. Those clues together indicate that Door 3 is the correct door to enter the next room.

**Page 37: Evolving Doors, The Fourth Room**

Let's look at Door 1's first statement. First, consider the question, "Would Door 3 say that Door 4 was a liar?"

| Door 3: | Door 4: |
| --- | --- |
| Truth-teller | Truth-teller |
| "No" | |

| Door 3: | Door 4: |
| --- | --- |
| Truth-teller | Liar |
| "Yes" | |

| Door 3: | Door 4: |
| --- | --- |
| Liar | Truth-teller |
| "Yes" | |

| Door 3: | Door 4: |
| --- | --- |
| Liar | Liar |
| "No" | |

Now we expand the table to include the question, "What would Door 2 say that Door 3 said?" (Note that Doors 2, 3, and 4 cannot be all truth-tellers or all liars, since there are exactly two truth-tellers and two liars.)

| Door 2: | Door 3: | Door 4: |
| --- | --- | --- |
| Liar | Truth-teller | Truth-teller |
| "Yes" | "No" | |

| Door 2: | Door 3: | Door 4: |
| --- | --- | --- |
| Liar | Truth-teller | Liar |
| "No" | "Yes" | |

| Door 2: | Door 3: | Door 4: |
| --- | --- | --- |
| Truth-teller | Truth-teller | Liar |
| "Yes" | "Yes" | |

| Door 2: | Door 3: | Door 4: |
| --- | --- | --- |
| Liar | Liar | Truth-teller |
| "No" | "Yes" | |

| Door 2: | Door 3: | Door 4: |
| --- | --- | --- |
| Truth-teller | Liar | Truth-teller |
| "Yes" | "Yes" | |

| Door 2: | Door 3: | Door 4: |
| --- | --- | --- |
| Truth-teller | Liar | Liar |
| "No" | "No" | |

Let's expand the table further to include Door 1 (since it's determined by elimination), and add what Door 4 would report that Door 2 had said. Also, remember that this statement about what Door 2 said is being made by Door 1, so we'll indicate whether it's possible or not for Door 1 to make such a statement.

| Door 1: | Door 2: | Door 3: | Door 4: |
| --- | --- | --- | --- |
| Liar | Liar | Truth-teller | Truth-teller |
| possible | "Yes" | "No" | "Yes" |

| Door 1: | Door 2: | Door 3: | Door 4: |
| --- | --- | --- | --- |
| Truth-teller | Liar | Truth-teller | Liar |
| impossible | "No" | "Yes" | "Yes" |

| Door 1: | Door 2: | Door 3: | Door 4: |
| --- | --- | --- | --- |
| Liar | Truth-teller | Truth-teller | Liar |
| impossible | "Yes" | "Yes" | "No" |

| Door 1: | Door 2: | Door 3: | Door 4: |
| --- | --- | --- | --- |
| Truth-teller | Liar | Liar | Truth-teller |
| possible | "No" | "Yes" | "No" |

| Door 1: | Door 2: | Door 3: | Door 4: |
| --- | --- | --- | --- |
| Liar | Truth-teller | Liar | Truth-teller |
| possible | "Yes" | "Yes" | "Yes" |

| Door 1: | Door 2: | Door 3: | Door 4: |
| --- | --- | --- | --- |
| Truth-teller | Truth-teller | Liar | Liar |
| impossible | "No" | "No" | "Yes" |

We've therefore narrowed our options to three:

| Door 1: | Door 2: | Door 3: | Door 4: |
| --- | --- | --- | --- |
| Liar | Liar | Truth-teller | Truth-teller |

| Door 1: | Door 2: | Door 3: | Door 4: |
| --- | --- | --- | --- |
| Truth-teller | Liar | Liar | Truth-teller |

| Door 1: | Door 2: | Door 3: | Door 4: |
| --- | --- | --- | --- |
| Liar | Truth-teller | Liar | Truth-teller |

For convenience we will refer to these as LLTT, TLLT, and LTLT. Now let's consider Door 2's first statement. There are three doors involved in the chain of statements: Door 2 reporting what Door 1 would say Door 4 had said. If an even number of those doors are liars, the answer given will be true, because the liars' responses will cancel each other out, no matter what order they are in. Scenario LLTT has two liars in the chain, which would mean the "yes" response was true, so for LLTT, Door 1 or 2 is correct. TLLT and LTLT both have only one liar in the chain, which would make the "yes" answer false; for TLLT and LTLT, then, Door 3 or 4 is correct.

As for Door 3's first statement, the chain of statements (Door 3 reporting what Door 4 would say Door 1 had said) can either include one liar (LLTT, TLLT) or two (LTLT). With one liar, the answer "yes" is false, so for the LLTT and TLLT scenarios, the correct door is Door 2 or 4; with two liars, the answer "yes" is true, so for the LTLT scenario, the correct door is Door 1 or 3.

Combining the information from the paragraphs above, we can see that each scenario is narrowed down to one correct door: for LLTT, Door 2 is correct; for TLLT, Door 4 is correct; and for LTLT, Door 3 is correct.

We now look at Door 4's first statement. We know it's true, because Door 4 is a truth-teller in all scenarios. Let's see what the responses would be for all three possibilities. For LLTT, since Door 2 is correct, Door 1 would lie and say it wasn't, and Door 2 would lie and say Door 1's response was "yes"; this option is, therefore, not possible. For TLLT, since Door 4 is correct, Door 1 would truthfully answer "no," and Door 2 would lie and say Door 1 had said "yes"; this option is also not possible. As for LTLT, since Door 3 is correct, Door 1 would lie and say it wasn't, and Door 2 would truthfully say Door 1 had answered "no." This, then, is the correct scenario: Doors 1 and 3 are liars, Doors 2 and 4 are truth-tellers, and Door 3 is the correct door. The combination is the product of the primes on the two truth-telling doors, $89 \times 71 = 6319$.

**Page 38: Evolving Doors, The Fifth Room**

If the oval plaque is true, Door 2's first statement is false (since the trapezoidal plaque is false), which makes Door 1's statement true. Since the oval plaque states only one door is a truth-teller, Doors 3 and 4 must be liars. However, both their statements are true (the oval plaque is true and door 4 is a liar; and Doors 2 and 3 are both liars), so this is impossible.

If the rectangular plaque is true, Door 1's and Door 2's first statements are both false. The rectangular plaque states there are exactly two liars, so Doors 3 and 4 must be truth-tellers. Door 3's first statement is indeed true (the oval plaque is a liar and Door 4 tells the truth), but Door 4's first statement is false (Door 2 is a liar and Door 3 tells the truth), so this is also impossible.

**79**

By elimination, the trapezoidal plaque must be true, and so only one door is a liar. If Door 2 is lying, since the trapezoidal plaque is true, the only way for Door 2's first statement to be false is if Door 3 is also a liar, which is impossible, so Door 2 is telling the truth. This makes Door 1's first statement false, so Door 1 is the liar, and Doors 3 and 4 are truth-tellers. Just to confirm, let's check Doors 3 and 4's first statements. The oval plaque is lying and Door 4 tells the truth, so Door 3's statement is true, and Doors 2 and 3 are both truth-tellers, so Door 4's statement is true.

Which door is the correct door? Door 1 is lying, so the statement "The correct door is mentioned by name by fewer than two other doors" is false, and the correct door must have been mentioned at least twice. Door 2 is mentioned by Doors 1 and 4, and Door 3 is mentioned by Doors 2 and 4, so the correct door is either Door 2 or Door 3. Door 2's statement "The correct door does not mention a plaque that is a liar" is true. The oval and rectangular plaques are liars, and they are mentioned by Doors 1 and 3; eliminating Door 3 means that Door 2 is the correct door.

Now to figure out the five-letter password. Door 1's false statements about the password mean that password contains at least one of the letters in DELAY and at least one of the letters in VODKA, and all the other statements about the passwords are true. Now consider these facts:

- The password contains at least one of the letters in DELAY.
- The password contains at least two of the letters in VIRUS.
- The password contains at least two of the letters in NOTCH.

These three words have no letters in common, so since the password contains only five letters, the password must contain exactly those numbers of letters from each word (that is, exactly one from DELAY, exactly two from VIRUS, and exactly two from NOTCH). The password contains none of the letters in SMART or SALON, so we can eliminate those, which leaves us with this:

- The password contains exactly one of the letters D, E, and Y.
- The password contains at least two of the letters V, I, and U.
- The password contains the letters C and H.

We also know the password contains at least one of the letters in GNOME; that letter can only be E. It also contains at least one of the letters in VODKA, which could be D or V, but the E already accounts for the one letter from DELAY, so it's V. Finally, the password contains at least one of the letters in LINTY; that could be I or Y, but, again, no more letters from DELAY are used, so the final letter must be I. The letters C, E, H, I, and V anagram to only one word: the password, CHIVE, entered into Door 2.

**Page 39: Evolving Doors, The Final Room**

For convenience, let's label the signs A, B, and C from left to right. Remember that even if a sign mentions a door by name, it may be hanging on that door.

First, consider sign B's second statement. The alternator can never say "My previous statement was true"; either it will truthfully report that its previous statement was a lie, or it will lie and say that its previous true statement was false. Therefore sign B is the truth-teller or the liar.

Bearing that in mind, we will now examine the implications of each sign's first statement.

Sign A: Door 1 is the alternator.
Sign B: Door 3 is the truth-teller.
Sign C: Door 2 is the liar.

Let's assume sign B is the truth-teller; in that case, sign B must be on Door 3 (since sign B's first statement is true). If sign C is the liar, then its statement that Door 2 is the liar is false, so sign C is on Door 1. Sign A, by elimination, is the alternator and is on door 2 (and its first statement is false, since we know door 1 is the liar, not the alternator). If sign A is the liar, then its statement that Door 1 is the alternator is false, so sign A is on Door 1. Sign C, by elimination, is the alternator and is on door 2 (and its first statement is false). We have, then, these two possibilities so far:

| Door 1: | Door 2: | Door 3: |
|---|---|---|
| C | A | B |
| Liar | Alternator | Truth-teller |

| Door 1: | Door 2: | Door 3: |
|---|---|---|
| A | C | B |
| Liar | Alternator | Truth-teller |

Let's now assume sign B is the liar. If sign A is the truth-teller, then it's true that Door 1 is the alternator, who can only be sign C. Sign B is lying about Door 3 being the truth-teller, so sign A can't be on Door 3 and must be on Door 2 (which makes sign C's first sentence false), with sign B on Door 3. If sign C is the truth-teller, then it's true that Door 2 is the liar, so sign B is on Door 2. Since sign B is lying about Door 3 being the truth-teller, sign C must be on Door 1. By elimination, sign A is the alternator and is on Door 3 (and its first statement is false). We now have these two additional possibilities:

| Door 1: | Door 2: | Door 3: |
|---|---|---|
| C | A | B |
| Alternator | Truth-teller | Liar |

| Door 1: | Door 2: | Door 3: |
|---|---|---|
| C | B | A |
| Truth-teller | Liar | Alternator |

In every case, the alternator's first statement is false, so its second statement will be true. Let's now go through all four of the above possibilities and compare them to sign A's second statement ("The truth-teller's door is the correct door") and sign C's second statement ("The alternator's door is correct and/or Door 3 is correct") to see which doors could be correct per those statements and their truth value. (Remember that, for this statement, the alternator will be telling the truth.)

| Door 1: | Door 2: | Door 3: |
|---|---|---|
| C | A | B |
| Liar | Alternator | Truth-teller |
| Door 1 | Door 3 | |

| Door 1: | Door 2: | Door 3: |
|---|---|---|
| A | C | B |
| Liar | Alternator | Truth-teller |
| Door 1 or 2 | Door 2 or 3 | |

| Door 1: | Door 2: | Door 3: |
|---|---|---|
| C | A | B |
| Alternator | Truth-teller | Liar |
| Door 1 or 3 | Door 2 | |

| Door 1: | Door 2: | Door 3: |
|---|---|---|
| C | B | A |
| Truth-teller | Liar | Alternator |
| Door 3 | | Door 1 |

Only in the second of these situations is there any door that Sign A and Sign C agree can be the correct one, and so that is the correct assignment of signs to doors, and the correct door is Door 2. Door 1/Sign A is the liar, Door 2/Sign C is the alternator, and Door 3/Sign B is the truth-teller.

Now to determine which key to use. Door 1/Sign A is the liar, so the correct key is not red, orange, or yellow. Door 2/Sign C is the alternator and told the truth in its second statement, so its third statement is a lie, and the correct key is not red, blue, or green. Door 3/Sign B is the truth-teller, so the correct key is green, orange, or purple—but the other two signs have eliminated orange and green as possibilities, so the correct key is purple.

**Pages 40–41: Card-Carrying Puzzlers**

If the lowest hand was a pair and every poker hand was accounted for (clue 2), then every possible poker hand better than nothing was held by someone: one pair, two pair, three of a kind, straight, flush, full house, four of a kind, and straight flush. The straight flush was a royal flush (clue 2), so it was 10 through ace in some suit, therefore the four of a kind was 9's or lower. Since the straight held no face cards (clue 3), it was 5–9 or 6–10. The four of a kind, then, can't have been 6's, 7's, 8's, or 9's, or it would interrupt the straight by using up all four cards of one of the ranks the straight must include, so the four of a kind was four 5's, and the straight was 6–10, and includes the 9 of clubs (since the straight contains no red cards, per clue 3, and Ahmad has the 9 of spades, per clue 8).

Since the straight included a 7, Greg or Olga had the straight (clue 5). Whichever one didn't have the straight held three 7's, so they had either a full house or three of a kind. But consider clue 11; Greg and Olga each had exactly one 8, and a full house can't contain only one 8. So neither Greg nor Olga held a full house, and since Greg's hand was higher than Olga's (clue 11), Greg had the straight and Olga had three of a kind, which was three 7's. Olga held the 7 of hearts and 7 of diamonds, since neither was in Greg's straight (clue 3). Malik and Ciara's hands ranked higher than a straight, with Malik's being the higher hand, and each contained a single 8 (clue 11). As already noted, a full house can't contain a single 8, and a royal flush doesn't contain any card lower than a 10, so Malik had four of a kind (which we already know was four 5's) and Ciara had a flush. Malik's 8 was the 8 of hearts (clue 10).

Ciara's flush includes no 5's (which are all in the four of a kind), no 7's (which are all held by Greg and Olga), no 10's (per clue 9), and no aces (which are in the royal flush and, per clue 6, somewhere among the four lowest hands), so that leaves only 6 ranks that could be part of the flush: 6, 8, 9, J, Q, and K. Per clue 7, only two cards in the flush have consecutive ranks, and those six cards contain three such pairs of cards: 8-9, J-Q, and Q-K. so one card must be removed to eliminate two of those pairs, and that card can only be the queen, so the flush is 6-8-9-J-K. Since both black 9's are accounted for, the flush is hearts or diamonds.

Of the people whose hands are not yet assigned, who had a royal flush? Not Ewan or Ichiko (since they can only make a royal flush by combining their cards), nor Ahmad (clue 8), so by elimination Kamala had a royal flush, and it was in hearts (clue 13). That means Ciara's flush can't have been in hearts (since it contained a jack and king), so it was in diamonds.

Ahmad didn't have a full house because neither his ace or his 9 could be part of three of a kind. Holding three aces isn't possible for Ahmad because Kamala has one ace, and Ewan or Ichiko has at least one other, per clue 4; holding three 9's is impossible because Ciara's flush and Greg's straight both include 9's. So Ewan or Ichiko had the full house, but since Ewan's hand was higher than Ichiko's (clue 4), Ewan had the full house. Ahmad and Ichiko, then, held two pair and one pair, in some order.

Who can have held the king of spades? Obviously not Kamala, Malik, or Ciara, whose hands we know in full. Not Greg, in whose full house the king would be part of a pair, and whoever had the king of spades held no other card higher than a 10 (clue 14). Not Greg, whose straight included no card higher than 10. Ahmad and Ichiko can't have held it either; Ahmad had the ace of diamonds (clue 8), and Ichiko needs to have held at least two cards higher than 10 to make a royal flush with Ewan (clue 4), who had a full house and held cards of only two ranks. Therefore the king of spades was one of the kickers in Olga's three of a kind. Olga's other kicker was an 8 (as we learned from clue 11), so that 8 was the 8 of spades (clue 12), and by elimination, Greg's straight contained the 8 of clubs. Olga's three of a kind didn't include any cards of the same suit as her kickers (clue 12), so her third 7 was the 7 of clubs, and the 7 of spades was in Greg's straight. Let's take a look at which cards we know the location of so far.

|  | 5 | 6 | 7 | 8 | 9 | 10 | J | Q | K | A |
|---|---|---|---|---|---|---|---|---|---|---|
| ♠ | M | | G | O | A | | | | O | |
| ♥ | M | | O | M | K | K | K | K | K | |
| ♣ | M | | O | G | G | | | | | |
| ♦ | M | C | O | C | C | | C | | C | A |

Ewan and Ichiko's royal flush can only have been in clubs, so Greg's 10 was the 10 of spades; we still don't know which of the black 6's Greg held. Ewan's three of a kind can only have been the three remaining queens. Ichiko can't have held two pair, because to complete the royal flush she must have held three clubs, and one of those clubs would be left over as the kicker, but the player with two pair had a spade kicker (clue 12), so Ichiko held one pair and Ahmad held two pair.

(The solution continues on the next page.)

For reference, here is the updated card grid:

|   | 5 | 6 | 7 | 8 | 9 | 10 | J | Q | K | A |
|---|---|---|---|---|---|----|---|---|---|---|
| ♠ | M |   | G | O | A | G |   |   | E | O |
| ♥ | M |   | O | M |   |    | K | K | K | K |
| ♣ | M |   | O | G | G | E or I | E or I | E | E or I | E or I |
| ♦ | M | C | O | C | C |    |   | C | E | C | A |

Ichiko's one pair didn't include any of the cards needed for the royal flush or the 6 of clubs (clue 15), so the pair can only have been the 6 of hearts and the 6 of spades, and by elimination the final card in Greg's straight is the 6 of clubs. The ace in Greg and Ichiko's royal flush must be held by Ichiko (clue 6). She doesn't have the other remaining ace (since she only has one pair) so Ahmad has the ace of spades. Ahmad's second pair can only have been 9's, so he also held the 9 of hearts. The suit of his kicker must match Olga's, so it's the only remaining spade: the jack of spades. This leaves the 10 of diamonds and the 10 of clubs as the only possible pair in Ewan's full house, so the king and jack of clubs are held by Ichiko.

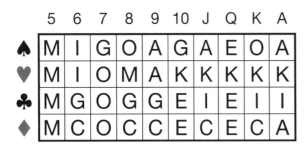

In summary:

Kamala held a royal flush: ♥A ♥K ♥Q ♥J ♥10.
Malik held four of a kind: ♠5 ♥5 ♣5 ♦5 ♥8.
Ewan held a full house: ♠Q ♣Q ♦Q ♣10 ♦10.
Ciara held a flush: ♦K ♦J ♦9 ♦8 ♦6.
Greg held a straight: ♠10 ♣9 ♣8 ♠7 ♣6.
Olga held three of a kind: ♥7 ♣7 ♦7 ♠K ♠8.
Ahmad held two pair: ♠A ♦A ♠9 ♥9 ♠J.
Ichiko held one pair: ♠6 ♥6 ♠A ♣K ♣J.

Ichiko paid for Kamala's admission, Ahmad paid for Malik's, Olga paid for Ewan's, and Greg paid for Ciara's.

**Page 42: In a Case of Emergency**

The eight phrases are each an anagram of one of our solar system's eight planets, plus a number:

GNU THIEVES = VENUS + EIGHT
HUNT ERASURE = URANUS + THREE
MIXES CURRY = MERCURY + SIX
PUREE JOINT = JUPITER + ONE
RAZORS TUNE = SATURN + ZERO
RISEN MAN = MARS + NINE
STEER HAVEN = EARTH + SEVEN
UPTOWN TEEN = NEPTUNE + TWO

The position of the Sun on the lock suggests we should order the planets according to their relationship with the Sun, with the nearest number to the Sun corresponding to Mercury, the nearest planet to the Sun, and so on. So, from left to right, the associated planets will be Neptune, Uranus, Saturn, Jupiter, Mars, Earth, Venus, and Mercury. The corresponding numbers are two, three, zero, one, nine, seven, eight, and six, so the combination is 23019786.

**Page 43: Rosalie the Robot**

At least one connection is vertical, and at least one is horizontal (clue 2). Either vertical connection, R-I or O-E, eliminates both R-O and I-E as a horizontal connection, so there is only one horizontal connection: S-A, S-L, or A-L.

The connection S-A is not possible, because A and S are the alphabetically first and last letters represented on the panel, so if they were connected, both of the other cord's pairs of letters would fall alphabetically between them, contradicting clue 3. The connection S-L is also not possible, because, since that leaves only one consonant to be connected, one other connection will have to be between two vowels, contradicting clue 4. The horizontal connection, therefore, is A-L.

If O-E is a vertical connection, we have these two pairs:

Of the remaining letters, only I falls alphabetically between either pair, and the two known pairs' ranges overlap, making it impossible to fulfill clue 3. R-I is therefore the only vertical connection.

Once again, the two ranges overlap. Of the remaining possible connections (S-E and S-O), only S-E fulfills the conditions of clue 3, with the R-I pair falling within its range. The fully connected panel looks like this:

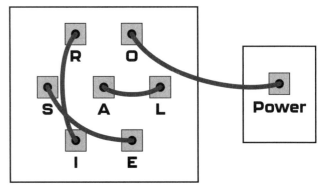

Reading the connected pairs from left to right, we have S-E, R-I, and A-L, which combine to spell SERIAL, which is the password to open the panel (and which is also a kind of port).

**Page 44: Star Search**

To solve the word search, the missing stars must be added to the word search grid to complete the phrases. For instance, you can make the phrase CUSTARD PIE in the top row of the grid by adding a star on top of the H in CUHDPIE. Below is the completed grid, with stars added in the appropriate locations to make the phrases easier to read:

The unused letters in the grid spell a hint about what to do next: "Look within the stars for the secret." If we read the letters that the stars have been placed upon, we get another message:

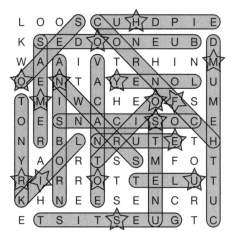

Those letters read HOMONYM OF "SERIOUS," a clue to the password, which is the star SIRIUS.

**Page 45: Constellation Prize**

All of the constellations can be labeled with letters, one letter per star, so that it's possible to spell one of the six mnemonic phrases by traveling from star to star along the lines of the constellation. Several of the mnemonics can be easily mapped by comparing the number of different letters in the phrases to the number of stars in the constellations. For instance, SPACE CAMP contains six different letters (ACEMPS), LUNAR COLONY contains eight different letters (ACLNORUY), and EXTRASOLAR PLANET contains ten different letters (AELNOPRSTX), so they correspond to the six-star, eight-star, and ten-star constellations, respectively.

In the phrase SPACE CAMP, S is only adjacent to one other letter (P), and E is also only adjacent to one other letter (C), so S and E must be at the endpoints of the constellation. Connecting the S to the E by writing in SPACE leaves only one place for the M to go, and since the M must connect to the A and P, that fixes the placement of the other letters.

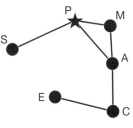

In the phrase LUNAR COLONY, Y is only adjacent to one other letter (N), so the Y is at the one endpoint of the constellation, connected to the N. There is also exactly one star with three paths connected to it; the only letter in the phrase adjacent to three other letters is O (adjacent to C, L, and N), so it corresponds to that star. The ARC sequence between N and O must travel along the outer curve, and then it's simple to place the L and U.

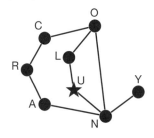

EXTRASOLAR PLANET is a little trickier, but we can use the same strategies. Only one star in the constellation has four paths leading to it, so we look for the letter in the phrase adjacent to the most letters: it's A (adjacent to L, N, R, and S). Two of the stars connected to the A have three paths leading to them, and the others have two paths. We therefore know that L (adjacent to A, O, and P) and R (adjacent to A, P, T) are the two three-path stars in some order, and N and S are the other two in some order. Also note the triangular shape in the lower left; it indicates that there is a pair of adjacent letters that are also the only two letters adjacent to another letter; this means we should examine the phrase for a letter that appears only once, and appears between a pair of letters that are adjacent elsewhere. That single letter is X, between E and T.

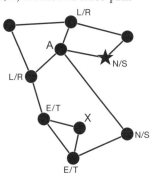

Looking at our options, we can see that the only way to spell EXTRA is if the E is at the bottom, with T and R above it; the star in the lower right must be N, which is only adjacent to A and E. The S and L are now placed by elimination, and must be connected by the O; the P goes with the remaining star.

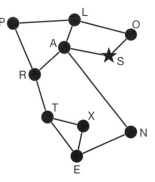

The remaining three phrases all contain 9 different letters, so we will need to figure out which one goes with which 9-star constellation.

**83**

IMPACT CRATERS is not too hard to pair up thanks to the IMP at the beginning: three letters that appear nowhere else in the phrase. This phrase must match the lower left constellation, which has a three-star-long endpoint, in which the IMP goes, connecting to an A. The S goes at the other endpoint, connecting to an R. The C must connect to both the A and R, and then filling in the rest of the letters is a simple matter.

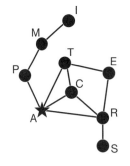

LAUNCH SEQUENCE starts with LA, two letters that appear nowhere else in the phrase. So, similarly to IMPACT CRATERS, those letters must appear in the two-star-long endpoint, connecting to U. The Q must connect to the U (by the path that leads down to the right, since Q is only adjacent to two letters, and that is the only adjoining star with exactly two paths), and then the other path leading from the Q connects with E. This leaves only one route to write in the first seven letters of the phrase, around the outer curve.

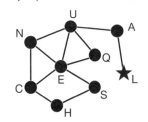

By elimination, the diagram in the upper left goes with AMATEUR ASTRONOMER. The only letter that can go in the endpoint is N, which is adjacent to only one letter, the O. The O connects to only two other letters: M by the path to the left, and R by the path to the right (since R is adjacent to more letters than M is). Of the letters that R is adjacent to, only the U appears in the phrase just once, so it's the letter of the only two-path star connected to the R.

The other path from the U connects to E, which connects to a T above. The A and S go in the remaining two stars, with the A above the S (since the A is adjacent to M and R in the phrase), and our constellation is completed.

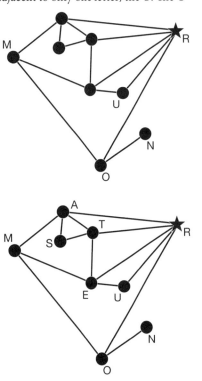

Now—what is the password? You probably noticed that each constellation diagram includes a single five-pointed star. Reading clockwise starting from the diagram in the upper middle (SPACE CAMP, LUNAR COLONY, LAUNCH SEQUENCE, EXTRASOLAR PLANET, IMPACT CRATERS, AMATEUR ASTRONOMER), and taking the letter associated with the star in each diagram, spells the password, PULSAR.

**Pages 46–47: You Could've Fueled Me**

As we solve through these grids, we'll tentatively indicate pipes with black lines until we know every pipe connection in a given square, at which point we'll replace it with a pipe piece. Every square contains a pipe, so the upper right and lower left corners contain L pipes. The other two corners have multiple options for the pipes they can contain, since they connect to incoming and outgoing pipes, but in this case, the clues indicate that they both contain the corner of a interior area, so they contain T tiles. Also, since the given pipe near the lower left corner doesn't connect to the square below it, that lower square must contain a horizontal pipe. We'll place the pipes we know and extend them into the adjacent squares.

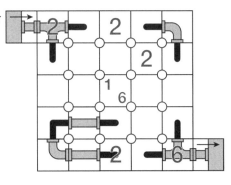

The 6 area doesn't touch the 2 clue at the bottom, so both of the 6 area's pipes must extend upward. The 6 area cannot connect along the right side to the pipe in the upper right corner, or it would include the circle in the lower right corner of the 2 clue in row 2, column 4, which is impossible (otherwise that square would contain both a 2 and 6 clue). So the 6 area must extend to the left after going up. As for the 2 area at the bottom, two circles are already contained in it, so it cannot extend further, and so we can add a pipe segment going up from the 2 clue. That makes three connections in the square above the 2, which is the maximum a square can have, so we can place the pipe in that square.

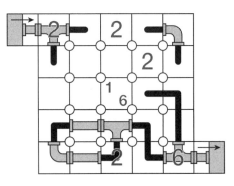

The 1 clue indicates that square contains the corner of a 2×2 loop. The 1 area can't extend down (since the square below it can't accept any more connections) or up to the right (since the 1 area doesn't enter that square), so it extends up and to the left. The 6 area still can't touch the 2 clue in the upper right, so it continues extending to the left. In fact, to reach 6 circles, it must continue all the way to the left side of the grid and up, where it stops before reaching the 2 clue, as shown. Several more squares can now take no more pipe segments; those are shown.

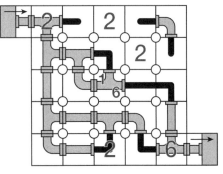

Actually, there can also be no more pipes extending from the square with the 2 clue along the bottom edge. If another pipe extended from it to the right, that would create a 1 area to its right, which contradicts the clue. So those squares are also fixed. The 2 clue in the upper left extends one more column to the right, connecting to the other 2 clue and sealing off. Similarly to the 2 clue on the bottom row, that 2 square can't contain an extension to its right, since it only contains part of one enclosed area. The

square to its right, then, extends down to the other 2 clue, which we can complete by extending one row further down. No more connections are possible, and the grid is complete.

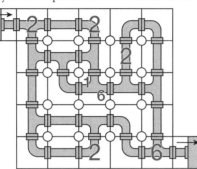

We'll move through the opening steps more quickly in the next one. We can start by placing L pipes in the upper right and lower left corners, extending the given pipe segment, and adding a I pipe to its left. The upper right L connects to the 1 clue; we can complete that 1 region right away, and since the 1 clue contains no part of any other region, it acts as a wall forming a corner for the clue below it, in which we can add another L tile. The clues along the edge that contain two numbers must contain T pipes. When we extend lines out from those T's, we get the starts of some enclosed regions, which must both extend along the edges

of the grid or they will be closed off too soon. Of the 2 and 6 regions extending from the T in the lower right, the 2 cannot be on the left, because it can't touch the 4/6 square; we can add a line to complete that area (and add completed pipe segments).

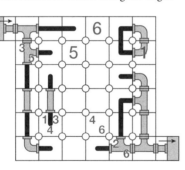

Whether it's the 3 or 5 region extending from the upper left corner, it doesn't touch the 6, so we can add two L tiles where they meet. This connects the upper left region with the 5 clue; the line to the left of the 5 clue can't extend to the right or it would close off the 5 area too soon, so it extends down. With that extension, the 3 region now contains all 3 of its circles, so we can close it off; that region also accounts for the 3 clue in the 1/3/4 square. The 1 region doesn't extend up (since an I tile is above), or down to the right (or it would create a second 1 region to its left) so the 1 region is in the corner. We've reached the maximum number

of connections in the 1/3/4 square, so the 4 area extends to the bottom of the grid. The 5 area doesn't touch the 1/3/4 square, so it must branch off above it, and it can't branch off from the I pipe, so it extends from the square above that pipe.

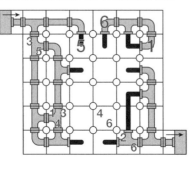

The 5 region isn't large enough yet, so it extends to the right, and the 6 area extends down. That in turn pushes the 5 region down

one more row, where we can close it off. The 6 region must extend to the bottom of the grid. The last enclosed area to complete is the 4 region, and there is only one way it's possible to do it without creating an extra region adjoining the 4/6 square.

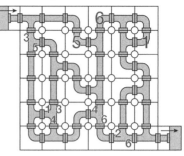

On to the 7×7 grid. Besides the usual starting steps (corners, blocked-off edge squares, pipe extensions), we also know that the 2 and 5 clues in the lower left each have regions that don't extend

into the other's square; likewise for the 5 and 3 clues along the bottom edge. This means we can treat those clues as if they have a wall between them. Along the bottom edge, we add L pipes, and in the lower left corner, there's only one way to complete the 2 area.

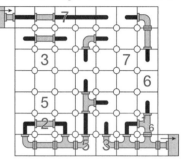

Let's look at the 7 and 6 clues on the right. The 6 clue is a single clue, so its square doesn't contain a T tile. It can't contain an I tile either, because then its region would include circles adjoining the 7 clue. This means we can add two more L pipes facing away from each other along the wall, in the 6 clue and the square above it.

There's only one way to complete the 3 region on the bottom edge without touching the 1/6 square or cutting off the 6 region. The 6 region must extend left to avoid touching the square with the 7 clue, then up, since it's too early to close the region off. There's

also only one way to complete the 5 region in the lower left; it must extend up so it doesn't touch the 2 clue, but not high enough to touch the 3 clue. (The two new L pipes along the left wall do not connect or they would create another region touching both the 2 and 5 clues.)

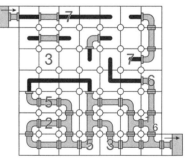

The square above the 7 clue must have at least two pipe segments extending from it, but it can't have segments extending both up and down or it would create a 2 area adjoining the 7 clue, as shown. So one pipe segment must extend from it to the left. The pipes extending along the top edge of the grid from the other 7 clue must continue extending to the right, or the two 7's will be cut off from each other, and there isn't room for them to be separate regions. A pipe must therefore extend up from the 7 clue on the right. The grid so far can be seen on the next page.

Now, what about the two leftmost squares in the top row? Can they be part of the 7 area? They cannot, because they extend its border too far, and it will be impossible to close the loop without including more than 7 circles. The border of the 7 area therefore extends straight down from the 7 clue on the top row to the edge of the 5 area, and we can also complete the 6 area by extending it one row up. Finally, there is only one way to complete the remaining 3 area without creating an additional enclosed 2×2 area adjoining the 3 clue. The completed grid is shown above right.

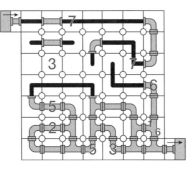

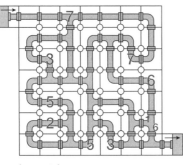

To find the password, we count the number of the indicated tiles used in each grid, and perform the given operations. In the first grid, there are 8 L tiles and 10 T tiles; 8×2=16 and 8+10=18. In the second grid, There are 15 L tiles and 14 T tiles; 15=15 (obviously) and (15×2)−14=16. In the third grid, there are 19 L tiles, 14 T tiles, and 16 I tiles; 19−14=5 and (14×2)−16=12. So we have the numbers 16, 18, 15, 16, 5, and 12, but we're looking for a word. Taking the 16th letter of the alphabet, then the 18th, and so on, spells PROPEL, the password.

### Pages 48–49: Landing of the Lost

The complete landing sequence, correctly ordered, is as follows:

When the dials are first set, they are pointing to the letters S, R, A, and E. The first instruction tells us to "set the sliders to another term for a flying saucer, except with the last letter changed to another letter you can make by erasing part of it." Erasing part of the O in UFO makes the letter C; we set the sliders to UFC to spell SURFACE (which, appropriately enough, is our destination).

Next, we turn the first dial two letters counterclockwise, changing S to A, then set the sliders to the notes in a C major triad (C, E, G) to spell ACREAGE.

Next, we turn the first and third dials two letters clockwise (changing the first A to S and the second A to P), then set the sliders to the end of Captain Picard's first name, spelled backward. His first name is Jean-Luc, so we set the sliders to CUL, spelling SCRUPLE.

Next, we turn the second dial two letters clockwise and the fourth dial to the opposite letter (changing R to U and E to R), then deactivate the first slider and set the other two to a college degree. The only college degree that completes a word is B.A., spelling SUBPAR. (No, P.E. is not a degree.)

Next we turn the fourth dial to the opposite letter (changing R to E). then set the sliders to another name for a vinyl record, spelled backward. Another name for a vinyl record is an LP, so we set the sliders to PL to spell SUPPLE.

Next, we turn the first dial one letter clockwise and the third dial two letters counterclockwise (changing S to E and P to A), then reactivate the first slider and set the sliders to the abbreviation for Connecticut, preceded by the last letter of its capital. The abbreviation for Connecticut is CT and its capital is Hartford, so we set the sliders to DCT to spell EDUCATE.

Next, we turn the first and second dials one letter clockwise (changing E to R and U to F), then set the sliders to the French word for "sea," with the first letter moved to the end. "Sea" in French is "mer," so we set the sliders to ERM to spell REFRAME.

Next, we turn the third dial one letter clockwise (changing A to R), then set the second and third sliders so they match the first slider. The first slider is currently set to E, so we set the other two sliders to E as well to spell REFEREE.

Next, we turn the first dial one letter clockwise and the fourth dial two letters counterclockwise (changing R to I and E to O), then change the first and third sliders to the compass point that's 90 degrees counterclockwise. They are set at E (east), and north is 90 degrees counterclockwise from east, so we set those two sliders to N to spell INFERNO.

Next, we turn the third and fourth dials two letters clockwise (changing R to U and O to E), then deactivate the second slider, and change the third slider to the opposite compass point. The opposite compass point from N (north) is south, so we set that slider to S to spell INFUSE.

Next, we turn the first dial two letters counterclockwise and the second dial one letter clockwise (changing I to E and F to U), then change the third slider from S to the previous letter in the alphabet, R, to spell ENSURE.

Next, we turn the third dial to the opposite letter and the fourth dial one letter clockwise (changing U to A and E to L), then reactivate the second slider and set it so it matches the slider to its left. The first slider is set to N, so we set the second slider to N as well to spell ENSNARL.

Next, we turn the second dial one letter clockwise and the fourth dial one letter counterclockwise (changing S to I and L to E), and set the sliders to one of the stars of "Rocky III." Mr. T played Rocky's opponent in "Rocky III," so we set the sliders to MRT to spell EMIRATE.

Next, we turn the first dial two letters counterclockwise and the third dial to the opposite letter (changing E to L and A to U), and set the sliders to the Phoenix Suns' sports league, shifted 17 letters ahead in the alphabet. The Suns play in the NBA, and NBA shifted 17 letters ahead is ESR, so we set the sliders to ESR to spell LEISURE.

Next, we turn the first dial to the opposite letter and the second dial one letter counterclockwise (changing L to R and I to S), then deactivate the third slider and set the other two sliders to a brain measurement. We set the first two sliders to IQ to spell RISQUE.

Next, we turn the second dial to the opposite letter and the third dial two letters clockwise (changing S to V and U to S), then set the sliders to an abbreviation meaning "that is," spelled backward. The abbreviation for "that is" is "i.e.," so we set the sliders to EI to spell REVISE.

Next, we turn the first dial two letters clockwise (changing R to A), then reactivate the third slider and set the sliders to a six-sided solid used in games. A cube used in games is a die, so we set the sliders to DIE to spell ADVISEE.

Next, we turn the second dial to the opposite letter and the third dial one letter counterclockwise (changing V to S and S to L), then set the sliders to a term for a male child, except with the last letter changed to another letter you can make by erasing part of it. Erasing part of the Y in BOY makes the letter V; we set the sliders to BOV to spell ABSOLVE.

Next, we turn the second dial two letters clockwise and the fourth dial one letter counterclockwise (changing S to R and E to C), and set the sliders to a word meaning "covered with frost," with the first letter moved to the end. A word meaning "covered with frost" is "icy," so we set the sliders to CYI to spell ACRYLIC.

Finally, we turn the third and fourth dials to the opposite letter (changing L to R and C to P) and set the sliders so they spell a phrase heard at a wedding. "I do" is a phrase heard at weddings, so we set the sliders to IDO to spell AIRDROP, which is the word to enter into the ship's computer to drop safely through the planet's air.

**Page 50: Basket Case**

The answers to the clues are TRIM, NEST, MISTS, BLACKBOARD, and WHOOP. Deleting a letter from each word gives you RIM, NET, MISS, BACKBOARD, and HOOP, These are the instructions for the "five perfect shots": hit the rim, hit the net, miss completely, hit the backboard, shoot through the hoop. Completing all five actions causes the game to dispense five orange tickets.

**Pages 50–51: Digits and Dragons**

By using standard sudoku logic, we can fill in only a few digits before getting stuck:

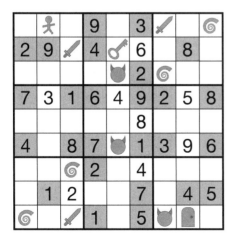

Instead, let's ignore the numbers briefly and figure out what path we'll need to take through the grid. No matter what, our path will start by picking up the sword. But then which direction do we turn? If we turn toward the left side of the grid, instead of turning toward the monster, we end up with the path seen here.

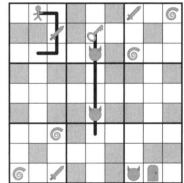

Since we can never revisit a square, that cuts off one of the three paths leading to the monster. And since we have to slay all the monsters before leaving, we'll need to pass through the monster's square, which there's now only one way to do. But the same thing is true of the monster directly below it: we will have to pass through that square, and there's only one way in and out of it. If we draw the paths through those monsters, we can see that they meet. This is impossible, because whichever direction that path travels, there's nowhere to pick up a sword between the monsters. Assuming you slayed the first monster, the sword was destroyed in the battle, so then you will have no weapon when you reach the other monster, and it will eat you. To avoid this, the path cannot travel down from that monster, and therefore your first turn must be toward it, slaying it with the sword you just picked up. You'll then grab the key and turn toward the right side of the grid, where you must pick the sword up or you'll never get another chance. From there you

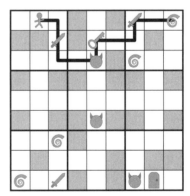

will teleport through the portal, but we don't yet know to where. We do know, however, that this sword will be used to slay the monster in row 6, because the monster in row 9 must be the last monster you slay, as it leads directly to the exit. The sword in row 9 is the sword you will use to slay that final monster.

Now let's use a combination of adventuring logic and sudoku logic. The numbers of the key and door must match. The only candidates remaining for the key are 1, 5, and 7, but the door can't be 1 or 5, so both are 7. That leaves two candidates for the first sword (3 and 5) and three candidates for the first monster (1, 5, and 8). If the monster is 5 or 8, it will be impossible for the sword to be strong enough to defeat it, since the highest candidate for the sword is a 5, and the sword must be more powerful than the monster. The monster, therefore, can only be 1. This lets us progress a little further with sudoku logic, getting us to the grid seen on the next page.

Once again we must study the dungeon layout. Take a look at the portal in row 1; the candidates for that cell are 4 and 7. Both 4 and 7 are eliminated as candidates for the portal in row 9, and 4 is eliminated as a candidate for the portal in row 7, so the only possibility is that the portals in row 1 and row 7 are both 7's—and the other two portals match, but we don't yet know what they are (they could be 6's or 9's). Let's also look at the sword and monster in row 9. The monster could be 6 or 8 (9 is not yet eliminated from that square by sudoku logic, but the monsters cannot be 9's or they would be impossible to defeat). The sword could be 3, 4, 6 or 9; but the 3, 4, and 6 would give you a sword too weak to defeat the monster in any case, so the sword must be a 9. This eliminates 9 as a possibility for the portal square, so the other portals contain 6's. Now that we know which portal is which, we can draw the complete path: you'll emerge from the portal in row 7 (going left, not

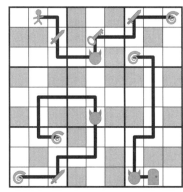

down, or you'll cut off the path to the sword), follow the path to the monster, then retrieve the last sword. From there you can only continue on to the other portal, emerging in row 3 and heading down to slay the last monster, unlock the door, and exit. The numbers we assigned in that step let us get quite far with sudoku logic, taking us almost all the way to the end, and the grid above.

At that point, in the center 3×3 region, the remaining candidates are 2 and 5. But we need to slay the monster in the sixth row with the 4-powered sword on our way past, so the monster must be weaker than the sword, which means it has to be a 2. That specifies all the remaining cells, and we're done!

As for what to enter on the high score screen, we have this set of symbols:

The door's value is 7. The combined value of all three swords is 3+4+9=16, and the combined value of all three monsters is 1+2+8=11; subtracting monsters from swords as indicated gives us 16−11=5. The key's value is 7, and your starting square is a 6; adding them together as indicated gives 7+6=13. Reading the alphabetic equivalents of 7, 5, and 13 gives us the word GEM. Entering that on the high score screen causes the machine to dispense seven blue tickets.

### Page 52, top: Tee Ceremony

The cities on the shirts are located in seven different states:

  Little Rock, Arkansas
  Santa Barbara, California
  Dover, Delaware
  Bar Harbor, Maine
  St. Louis, Missouri
  Newport, Rhode Island
  Mobile, Alabama

"State what you're looking at" suggests that the states are important. Reading the state abbreviations of those states in order, we get ARCADE MEMORIAL, which is, indeed, what you're looking at. Typing that in opens the case, which lets you retrieve a string of three purple tickets tucked into one of the shirts.

### Page 52, bottom: Taking the Plunger

The answers to the clues are JOIN, LIGHT, KITE, THEFT, SIGHT, HEFT, WEFT, KNIGHT, and BULL. These are rhymes for the series of actions to perform: COIN (insert token into slot), RIGHT (press right flipper), RIGHT, LEFT (press left flipper), RIGHT, LEFT, LEFT, RIGHT, PULL (pull plunger). Performing these actions causes the pinball machine to dispense eight yellow tickets.

### Page 53, top: It's All Downhill From Here

The final two digits of the high scores, translated into letters using A=1, B=2, etc., read JUST ROMAN. Looking at just the Roman numerals in the list of initials on the high score screen, we see, from top to bottom: L, X, I, CL, C, V, I, C, X, which are all values of Ski-Ball targets. Rolling the nine balls so that they score, in order, 50, 10, 1, 150, 100, 5, 1, 100, and 10 points causes the Ski-Ball machine to dispense six silver tickets.

**Page 53, bottom: The Long Arm of the Claw**

The names of the six plush toys can all be found hidden inside the other six items, minus a letter. The ALIEN is found in the C**ALIEN**DAR, minus an I. The APPLE is found in the ST**APLE**R, minus a P. The COYOTE is found in the S**COOTE**R, minus a Y. ERNIE is found in the GAME G**ENIE**, minus an R. The HERON is found in the JEEP C**HERO**KEE, minus an N. And ZURG is found in the map of **ZUR**ICH, minus a G.

Each of the plush items has a rainbow color: the apple is red, Ernie is orange, the coyote is yellow, the alien is green, the heron is blue, and Zurg is purple. Reading the missing letters above in rainbow order gives us the password PRYING, which allows us to open the access panel and retrieve five olive tickets.

**Page 54: Cheat Codes**

The names of the video games are all hidden in the grid, following winding paths. When matched up correctly, each cheat code provides a guide to the path each game takes in the grid. "Up," "down," "left," and "right" provide literal directions in the grid, while A and B represent the actual letters A and B, which do not appear in the grid.

For example, to spell DOUBLE DRAGON in the grid, Ahmad would place his cursor on the circled G in row 4, column 4, then he would follow this cheat code: left, left, up (DOU), press B, right, right, up, up (LEDR), press A, left, left, left (GON). All the correct pairings are:

CASTLEVANIA: left, A, left, down, down, down, right, A, down, left, A, start
COMBAT: up, up, right, B, A, right, start
CRAZY CLIMBER: right, down, A, down, left, up, left, left, down, B, down, left, start
DOUBLE DRAGON: left, left, up, B, right, right, up, up, A, left, left, left, start
EXCITEBIKE: left, down, right, right, up, up, B, up, left, left, start
GALAXIAN: up, A, up, A, up, up, A, right, start

GHOSTS 'N' GOBLINS: right, up, up, right, right, up, up, up, right, B, down, down, right, up, start
LUNAR LANDER: left, left, up, A, left, up, A, up, up, left, left, start
MANIAC MANSION: right, A, right, up, A, right, up, A, up, up, up, up, left, start
MARBLE MADNESS: left, A, up, B, up, right, up, A, left, up, up, up, right, start
METAL GEAR: right, up, right, A, down, down, left, A, left, start
MS. PAC-MAN: down, right, up, A, up, right, A, right, start
NINJA GAIDEN: down, left, left, down, A, right, A, right, right, right, down, start
PAPERBOY: left, A, up, up, left, B, up, right, start
PITFALL!: down, right, right, right, A, up, up, start
Q*BERT: up, B, up, right, right, start
RAMPAGE: up, A, up, up, A, left, left, start
ROBOTRON: up, right, B, up, right, right, right, up, start
SUPER MARIO BROS.: left, left, down, left, left, down, A, down, right, right, B, down, down, left, start

The note on the cheat codes, "Don't forget the 'start'!" is meant as a hint to make a note of the letters on which you have to start in order to successfully follow the cheat codes (for instance, the G we started with to spell DOUBLE DRAGON). Those "start" letters are circled in the answer grid. If you make a note of the correct start letter at the end of each cheat code, you can then read down the list of cheat codes to spell the message TEDIOUS SWEDISH GROUP. "Tedious" is a synonym for DULL, and ABBA is a Swedish group. DULL ABBA is shorthand for the cheat code "down, up, left, left, A, B, B, A," entering which causes the console to open to reveal six crimson tickets. (Please note that the above clue does not reflect the opinion of either author as regards the work of the band ABBA, who are great and not tedious at all.)

**Page 55: Counter Intuitive**

When correctly paired up with the "initials," the phone numbers spell 9-letter words, using the equivalent letters on the phone keypad for each number:

GL 477-2636 = GLISSANDO
RE 787-2468 = RESTRAINT
SI 989-3687 = SIXTY-FOUR
SO 548-2473 = SOLITAIRE
PA 567-7468 = PALMPRINT
HE 235-4448 = HEADLIGHT
IN 352-8466 = INFLATION
SM 255-8463 = SMALL-TIME
DI 748-4733 = DISGUISED

Each of these words can be paired up with one of the items from the prize counter. You can play a GLISSANDO on a slide whistle; a finger trap is a RESTRAINT; there are SIXTY-FOUR squares on a chessboard; playing cards can be used for SOLITAIRE; a sticky hand toy may leave a PALMPRINT behind; glowing glasses are literally a light you wear on your head, so, a HEADLIGHT; balloon INFLATION is involved in using a balloon animal kit; a miniature clock shows a SMALL TIME; and if you are wearing a fake moustache, you are DISGUISED.

(The solution continues on the next page.)

Looking at those nine prizes in the order of the words in the phone book, we have:

| | |
|---|---|
| 6 tickets — | slide whistle |
| 2 tickets — | finger trap |
| 6 tickets — | travel chess set |
| 11 tickets — | playing cards |
| 4 tickets — | sticky hand |
| 9 tickets — | glowing glasses |
| 8 tickets — | balloon animal kit |
| 4 tickets — | miniature clock |
| 5 tickets — | fake moustache |

Reading the 6th letter of SLIDE WHISTLE, the 2nd letter of FINGER TRAP, the 6th letter of TRAVEL CHESS SET, the 11th letter of PLAYING CARDS, and so on, we spell the phrase WILD CLAIM, the password that activates the automatic ticket redemption machine.

### Pages 56–57: That's the Ticket

The group of seven tickets in clue 12 must be either blue or yellow (the only two colors with seven or more tickets), but the seven tickets must be separated into at least two groups of five or less (per clue 1), and two sets of yellow tickets can't be within 10 tickets of each other (clue 5), so the seven tickets are blue. All the blue tickets, then, are contained within a single block of ten, but, per clue 7, not 1–10 (which would leave no room for the orange tickets to precede the blue tickets) or 31–40 (which would leave no room for the purple tickets to follow the blue tickets).

We know there are 15 sets in total (clue 1). The five orange tickets can't be in three or more sets without having two sets of the same length, contradicting clue 6; and they cannot be in a single set because then they would have to be adjacent to a purple ticket (clue 10), but the orange and purple tickets are separated by the blue tickets (clue 7). There are therefore two sets of orange tickets. The five olive tickets must also be in two sets, because one of the sets in clue 9 is olive, and none of those sets contains more than four tickets (1+2+3+4 is the only way for four numbers to add up to 10 without repeating a number). The three purple tickets can be in a single set, or in two sets (of 1 and 2).

If the blue tickets were in three groups, they would have to be divided into sets of 1, 2, and 4. Since there are only single tickets available to separate the blue groups from each other (clue 12), that would force the single blue ticket to be adjacent to another single ticket, and there are no adjacent sets of single tickets besides the ones in clue 13, which are in a different group of ten. The blue tickets are therefore in two groups.

There are six silver tickets; to fulfill clue 6, they can be divided into three sets of 1, 1, and 4; or two sets of 3 and 3. (Being divided into sets of 2, 2, and 2 is not possible, because that's three identical groups, and there are exactly two.) Whether there are three silver sets or two, the crimson tickets are divided into the same number of sets (clue 11).

So, we know there are two yellow sets (per clue 5), two orange sets, two olive sets, and two blue sets. That accounts for eight of the 15 sets. Then there's either 1 or 2 purple sets, and either 4 or 6 silver and crimson sets combined. But if there are only four silver and crimson sets combined, that's not enough to reach 15 even if

there are two purple sets, so there are three sets each of silver and crimson tickets, and only one purple set. The three sets of crimson tickets must be 1, 2, and 3 (since none are the same length, per clue 6).

Yellow's two sets of tickets are 3 and 5 (since they are not equal, per clue 6). Blue's are either 2 and 5, or 3 and 4. Purple is a single set of 3. That meaning the remaining colors—orange, silver, olive, and crimson—must account for the single tickets in clue 13. (The four tickets are all different colors, per clue 13, so only one of the two single-ticket silver sets can be included.) Therefore the olive and orange tickets are both in sets of 1 and 4.

Looking back at the sets in clue 12, the two sets of blue tickets must be interrupted by silver, the only other single ticket remaining; the other two tickets in the block must be the first and last tickets in the block, and must be the ends of longer sets. However long the blue sets are, the second and ninth tickets in the block (either #12 and #19, or #22 and #29) must be blue. But they can't be #22 and #29, which would contradict clue 4 in multiple ways (the two blue sets are different lengths, and one is the last ticket in its set), so the block containing the blue tickets is 11–20, with the start of one blue set at #12 and the end of the other at #19. Ticket #22 starts a new set (clue 4), so 20–21 is a set of two. That means the set after the second blue set isn't the purple set of three, and the purple set can't precede the first blue set (since all the blue tickets precede all the purple tickets, per clue 7). Since no blue set is adjacent to a purple set, neither blue set contains 5 tickets (clue 10), so the blue sets are 3 and 4. We now know the size of every set in the sequence; let's recap for ease of reference:

blue: 3 and 4
crimson: 1, 2, and 3
olive: 1 and 4
orange: 1 and 4
purple: 3
silver: 1, 1, and 4
yellow: 3 and 5

We've already shown that 20–21 is a set of two, and there's only one ticket color with a set of two: crimson. It and the adjacent blue set are two sets from clue 9; the adjacent single silver ticket must be another (all other single tickets are in the clue 13 block, which precedes the blue tickets per clue 7 since it contains the single orange ticket). That leaves the sets of three and four to be assigned. The other color in the sequence, olive, can only account for the set of four, so blue is the set of three, and we now know the full sequence from #12 to #25: 12–15 is four blue tickets; #16 is one silver ticket; 17–19 is three blue tickets, 20–21 is two crimson tickets, and 22–25 is four olive tickets.

Another set of four begins at #29 (clue 4). It can't be orange, because all the orange tickets precede all the blue ones (clue 7), so it's silver. The set of three purple tickets must follow the blue tickets (clue 7), and must be adjacent to a set of five (clue 10), but not adjacent to a silver ticket (clue 2). This can only be accomplished with the yellow set of five in 33–37 and the purple set in 38–40. (They cannot swap positions or the purple set would be adjacent to the silver set in 29–32.) One of the two remaining sets of three must go in 26–28; it can't be the yellow set, since that's too close to the yellow set of five (clue 5), so it's the crimson set.

Now to figure out the first 11 tickets. Per clue 8, since tickets 33–37 are yellow tickets, none of tickets 3–7 can be yellow tickets. The yellow set of three doesn't have room to fit before ticket #3. If it were in 8–10, that would make ticket #11 a single ticket, but we have already shown that ticket #11 is the last ticket of a longer set, so that's impossible too, and the yellow set of three must be 9–11.

The two pairs of single-ticket sets must be separated by the remaining set of four orange tickets. (If the two pairs were adjacent, a third identical adjacent pair would be created in the middle.) Therefore that orange set is tickets 3–6.

The single tickets remaining to be paired up are crimson, olive, orange, and silver. The silver ticket can't be in #1 or #2 since silver tickets are in #31 and #32 (clue 8), so it's in #7 or #8. The olive set at 22–25 is preceded by a crimson set, so the remaining single olive ticket must be preceded by the crimson ticket (clue 3). They can't be together in 7–8 since the silver ticket is one of those, so the crimson ticket is #1 and the olive ticket is #2. The other single ticket is an orange ticket, which must be separated from the orange set of four by another ticket, so the silver ticket is at #7 and the orange ticket at #8, and we now have the full sequence. In summary, the correct sequence is:

- 1 crimson ticket
- 1 olive ticket
- 4 orange tickets
- 1 silver ticket
- 1 orange ticket
- 3 yellow tickets
- 4 blue tickets
- 1 silver ticket
- 3 blue tickets
- 2 crimson tickets
- 4 olive tickets
- 3 crimson tickets
- 4 silver tickets
- 5 yellow tickets
- 3 purple tickets

Now, what about the password? If we use the number of tickets in each set as an index into the color of the tickets (i.e., one crimson ticket indicates to take the first letter of "crimson," and three yellow tickets indicates to take the third letter of "yellow"), we get:

- 1 crimson = C
- 1 olive = O
- 4 orange = N
- 1 silver = S
- 1 orange = O
- 3 yellow = L
- 4 blue = E
- 1 silver = S
- 3 blue = U
- 2 crimson = R
- 4 olive = V
- 3 crimson = I
- 4 silver = V
- 5 yellow = O
- 3 purple = R

Entering the phrase CONSOLE SURVIVOR opens the box, letting you retrieve the key to access the back room, and claim the surviving Pong console.

**Page 58: Epilogue**

The initial letters of Frieda's speech spell her idea for what the group should do now that they've solved all the escape rooms in town: WRITE NEW ESCAPE ROOMS.

# Combinations & Passwords

0123456789: Come on now.

0124: Not the combination.

0342159678: Trying this has no effect.

101001510015011050: No, but try looking at things a different way.

101510015051105: Sorry, no.

1024: This isn't correct.

1234: You shouldn't use this as your password and we didn't either.

12345: This is also not a good password and is not the combination.

1235097468: This doesn't work.

1240587693: This opens the frame to reveal a pirate hat and a false beard.

1245039678: This doesn't budge the lock at all.

1245876903: Not the right combination.

1345: The box continues to be a box.

1354: The box opens to reveal a gold key.

14-39-25: This unlocks nothing.

1501105010051051: No tickets come out.

154528347: That doesn't do anything at all.

16-37-25: This opens the safe to reveals two chess knights, a pink one and a gray one.

1899: Doesn't seem to be right.

1910: Nope.

2014: I regret to say this is not the combination.

2045: Sorry, friend.

2103459678: Not correct.

211597798: That doesn't work; I think you might have this all backward.

23019786: This opens the case and allows you to retrieve the forceps.

2430967851: This doesn't have any effect on the lock.

2439015678: Nothing happens when you try this.

2439015876: This isn't the correct combination.

2410: Try again.

25341: This isn't correct (but you might be on the right track).

25-38-37: Not the correct combination.

26-31-21: Sorry, but no.

26-31-35: Keep trying.

2649: Not a winning combo.

27156438: That doesn't do anything.

27901638: The lock doesn't budge.

27-34-36: I admire your optimism, but no.

28-33-37: Doesn't work.

29-19-37: No luck.

30-31-39: Not the combination.

31-11-36: This isn't the right answer.

31-29-38: The box stays closed.

31-36-37: Nothing happens.

316129965: That's not the combination.

32-38-36: The box opens to reveal a silver key.

32-27-29: Alas, no.

32-29-17: This doesn't do anything.

33-34-31: The box stays completely shut.

3147: The box opens to reveal you're just making up numbers now.

33-35-27: Annoyingly, nothing happens.

3421096785: This doesn't work.

35-20-23: Not correct.

35679: The lock stays resolutely locked.

3918: Those are definitely numbers, but they don't open the lock.

39756: This isn't correct.

4012: This unlocks the suitcase to reveal two chess knights, a green one and a purple one.

4210: This isn't the combination.

4210587693: That didn't do anything.

4215039678: No luck this time.

4312: Not successful.

4812: Nothing happens.

50101150015011050: That's correct, and you receive 6 silver tickets.

53769: This is not the correct combination (but you might be on the right track).

5442889: No, but it's 2333 squared, so that's cool.

542343279: This doesn't work.

5501150105100105: You seem like you're having fun, but this isn't right.

5715: Nope.

63975: Unfortunately, this isn't correct.

6518: This doesn't work.

6612: The lock stays locked.

6785012439: Nothing happens when you try this.

6785930124: This doesn't have any effect.

67953: Better luck next time.

6815: Nothing happens.

68791032: That's not correct, but if you reflect for a moment I think you'll come up with it.

6915: The box opens to reveal a blue key.

76395: This isn't it.

779925811: The lock makes an unhelpful "clunk" noise.

7851: No; I just put this here to take up space.

798721951: This isn't it.

83465172: Trying this combination doesn't do anything.

83610972: Sorry, that's not correct.

8418: That's the number the puzzle started with. Very optimistic, but no.

8769034215: Not a successful attempt.

8769305421: This doesn't work.

8913: Hmmmm, no.

897795112: This unlocks the safe, which contains two chess knights, a blue one and a yellow one.

9510: Nope.

95763: This opens the box's lock to reveal the book *Silent Spring*, by Rachel Carson.

9615: Try again.

97653: This doesn't open the lock.

9918: Nothing happens.

AEROSOL: This doesn't work on whatever you're trying to use it on.

AGITATE: Not one of the answers.

AIRDROP: That's correct.

ALARMING: Nothing happens.

ALERTS: Sorry, no.

ALTAIR: That's not the answer.

ARCADE: That's the first part of the answer.

ASTERISK: No, that isn't it.

AUTO PARTS: Nothing happens.

BACKBOARD: Hitting the backboard is correct.

BIG BOARD: The lock doesn't budge.

BIRCH LEG: This isn't a phrase you need.

BOOKS: This doesn't do anything.

BULB AURA: You'll need another idea.

CANDID: This isn't an answer.

CAPTURES: This opens the suitcase to reveal two chess knights, a gold one and a silver one.

CARDS: No progress is made by trying this.

CASTOR: That didn't work.

CHECKERS: This doesn't open anything.

CIRRUS: Not quite.

CORN CHEX: This one is a nothingburger.

COSTAR: That's no help.

CRATER: Nothing happens.

CROATIAN: The lock doesn't move at all.

CRRLRLLRP: Performing these actions causes the machine to dispense 8 yellow tickets.

DIAGONAL: This isn't correct, and I'm going on longer than necessary just to break things up a bit visually.

DOUBLOON: Sorry, no.

DULL ABBA: These actions open the console to reveal 6 crimson tickets.

DUNK: This isn't correct.

EYEPATCH: Nothing happens.

FEN: That doesn't work, unfortunately.

FOUL: This is not one of the answers.

GANYMEDE: I'm afraid not.

GEM: Entering this causes the machine to dispense 7 blue tickets.

GOLD COIN: This isn't correct.

GRABBY: Try again.

GROG CASK: The lock doesn't budge.

HOLBROOK: That's not anything.

HOOP: Shooting through the hoop as the final step gets you 5 orange tickets.

INCOME: I must declare that didn't make anything happen.

INVADE: No help there.

INVERSE: Nothing is accomplished with that.

ISRAEL: That doesn't open the lock.

JLKTSHWKB: No, but keep thinking about it.

JPG: The cursor just keeps blinking.

LASER: This isn't correct.

LAUD BARD: Button-mashing? That doesn't work.

LMFCWBDQF: This would be a very willful thing to guess. It is not correct.

MAINLAND: That's not an answer.

MANDARIN: Better luck next time.

MARINE: Sorry, that didn't work.

MEALTIME: Nothing happens when you try this.

MEG: That doesn't do anything.

MEMORIAL: That's the rest of the answer, opening the case and allowing you to reach a set of 3 purple tickets.

MIASMA: Like so many answers on these pages, this is also not correct.

MINUTE: Nope.

MISS: Missing completely is the correct action.

MORE PIT: How would that work?

MPG: That doesn't do anything.

MUSTACHE: Unfortunately, this isn't the password.

NAMASTE: This causes the computer monitor to pop open; it has two chess knights inside, a white one and a black one.

NATIONAL: Better luck with the next attempt.

NET: Hitting the net is correct.

NOTATES: No.

OILERS: This doesn't do anything.

ONE-HORSE: The lock doesn't open.

ONYX HOOP: This opens the chest, which contains a round onyx (clip-on) earring.

ORDEAL: No deal.

PAGES: This isn't the combination.

PASS: Not one of the answers you need.

PAWNSHOP: You'll have to try again.

PAYING: It stays locked.

PEN: Sorry, that's not it.

PHONE CALL: No response.

PICTURES: That isn't the password.

PIE CRUST: Nothing happens.

PLANET: That has no effect.

PLANKING: This opens the drawer to reveal two chess knights, an orange one and a red one.

PLANTING: Try again.

PLASMA: Better luck next time.

PLASTICS: Sorry, no.

PLAYMATE: This doesn't work.

PRIMES: That isn't an answer you need.

PROBES: You should keep trying.

PROMPT: That wasn't it.

PROPEL: This successfully reactivates the fuel system.

PROPER: Unfortunately, that's not correct.

PRYING: This opens the panel, behind which you find 5 olive tickets.

RAD BLURB: No, but if you know someone who wants to contribute a rad blurb to this book's second edition, we are open to suggestions.

REROUTE: Seems like that didn't work.

RIM: Hitting the rim is correct.

RING: This is not a correct answer.

RIP VAN WINKLE: Creative, but no.

RUBY RING: This isn't the answer.

RUSTLER: Nothing happens.

SAILOR: That's not correct.

SCABBARD: No luck this time.

SEA SNAKE: Not an answer you need.

SECRET: Keep trying.

SERIAL: This unlocks the panel to access the power button.

SHELF: Didn't work, sorry.

SHOCK: That's a word, but it's not the password.

SINKING: This isn't an answer that you need.

SIRIUS: This allows you to access the control panel.

SOLAR: That didn't accomplish anything.

SOURCE: That doesn't seem like it worked.

SPINE: You'll need to try something else.

SQUARES: That's not helpful.

STARVED: This fails to do anything.

STIRRUP: Sorry, this isn't correct.

STORY: The safe opens to reveal the book *Marjorie Morningstar*, by Herman Wouk.

TENACITY: Not a successful attempt.

TITLE: Regretfully, this accomplishes nothing.

TOURNEY: This causes a lack of things to occur.

TRYING: Well, that didn't work.

WILD CLAIM: This activates the machine.

WOODWORK: Whatever it is, it isn't this.

WORDS: Nothing happens.

WORLD MAP: Sorry, but this doesn't do anything.

# "Evolving Doors" Combinations & Passwords

Door 1, 1357: The door remains locked.

Door 1, 1359: Nothing happens.

Door 1, 1379: The doorknob rattles, but that's it.

Door 1, 1579: The door doesn't open.

Door 1, 3149: That doesn't work.

Door 1, 3337: Sadly, this doesn't do anything.

Door 1, 3579: That doesn't work.

Door 1, 4183: That's not correct.

Door 1, 4757: You'll have to try again.

Door 1, 5963: Nothing happens.

Door 1, 6319: Better luck next time.

Door 1, 7531: Nope.

Door 1, 9531: This isn't correct.

Door 1, 9731: That's not it.

Door 1, 9751: Try again.

Door 1, 9753: This doesn't accomplish anything.

Door 1, blue key: Nothing happens.

Door 1, CHIVE: The lock doesn't respond.

Door 1, CHOP: No luck.

Door 1, CHOW: That didn't work.

Door 1, CLAW: Nothing happens.

Door 1, CLOP: Sorry, try again.

Door 1, CURVY: This fails to work.

Door 1, GLASNOST: The door stays locked.

Door 1, GOALPOST: This doesn't work.

Door 1, green key: No luck.

Door 1, HAIKU: Nothing to report except "try again."

Door 1, LIGHT: This isn't successful.

Door 1, LYRIC: Sorry, but that didn't do it.

Door 1, MULCH: That didn't do it.

Door 1, NORTHERN: That's not correct.

Door 1, NOSTRILS: This didn't do anything.

Door 1, orange key: That isn't correct.

Door 1, PORTUGAL: Sorry, no.

Door 1, POSTCARD: Try something else.

Door 1, purple key: That wasn't a success.

Door 1, red key: The key doesn't do anything.

Door 1, SHAW: The door doesn't open.

Door 1, SHOP: Trying this is not a success.

Door 1, SHOW: That didn't work.

Door 1, SLAP: The lock doesn't respond.

Door 1, SLAW: Better luck next time.

Door 1, SLOP: That isn't correct.

Door 1, STALWART: No luck with that one.

Door 1, STRATEGO: This doesn't have any effect.

Door 1, yellow key: Better luck next time.

Door 2, 1357: The lock doesn't respond.

Door 2, 1359: This opens the door.

Door 2, 1379: Nothing happens.

Door 2, 1579: That doesn't open the lock.

Door 2, 3149: This attempt does not succeed.

Door 2, 3337: That's not it.

Door 2, 3579: Better luck next time.

Door 2, 4183: This is incorrect.

Door 2, 4757: The lock doesn't respond.

Door 2, 5963: No luck.

Door 2, 6319: I wish I had better news, but that didn't work.

Door 2, 7531: This isn't correct.

Door 2, 9531: Try again.

Door 2, 9731: Sorry, but no.

Door 2, 9751: Nothing happens.

Door 2, 9753: That didn't work.

Door 2, blue key: The key won't turn in the lock.

Door 2, CHIVE: This unlocks the door.

Door 2, CHOP: Not the answer.

Door 2, CHOW: This doesn't work.

Door 2, CLAW: You'll have to try something else.

Door 2, CLOP: The door stays locked.

Door 2, CURVY: That's not the right answer.

Door 2, GLASNOST: That fails to unlock the door.

Door 2, GOALPOST: Nothing happened.

Door 2, green key: That didn't do anything.

Door 2, HAIKU: This is not correct.

Door 2, LIGHT: This didn't do anything.

Door 2, LYRIC: The lock stays locked.

Door 2, MULCH: Better luck next time.

Door 2, NORTHERN: This isn't successful.

Door 2, NOSTRILS: That doesn't open the lock.

Door 2, orange key: No luck this time.

Door 2, PORTUGAL: The knob still doesn't turn.

Door 2, POSTCARD: Trying this doesn't work.

Door 2, purple key: This opens the door.

Door 2, red key: This doesn't work.

Door 2, SHAW: Better luck next time.

Door 2, SHOP: Sorry, but that's not it.

Door 2, SHOW: This isn't right.

Door 2, SLAP: Not a success.

Door 2, SLAW: The lock doesn't respond to this.

Door 2, SLOP: This doesn't do anything.

Door 2, STALWART: That's not it.

Door 2, STRATEGO: Better luck next time.

Door 2, yellow key: You can barely even jiggle the key; try again.

Door 3, 3149: The door stays locked.

Door 3, 3337: That wasn't the right thing to do.

Door 3, 4183: Sorry, no.

Door 3, 4757: Try again.

Door 3, 5963: That's not the correct answer.

Door 3, 6319: This opens the door successfully.

Door 3, blue key: This isn't it.

Door 3, CHIVE: Either that's the wrong password, or this is the wrong door, or both.

Door 3, CHOP: Alas, this is incorrect.

Door 3, CHOW: Nothing happens.

Door 3, CLAW: No luck.

Door 3, CLOP: This has no effect whatsoever.

Door 3, CURVY: I'm sorry to say that didn't work.

Door 3, GLASNOST: That didn't do anything.

Door 3, GOALPOST: This opens the door.

Door 3, green key: Sorry, but no.

Door 3, HAIKU: No luck with that one.

Door 3, LIGHT: Try again.

Door 3, LYRIC: That doesn't affect the lock.

Door 3, MULCH: That's not correct.

Door 3, NORTHERN: No luck with that one.

Door 3, NOSTRILS: Nothing happens.

Door 3, orange key: Try again.

Door 3, PORTUGAL: The goal of opening the door was not achieved.

Door 3, POSTCARD: This isn't it.

Door 3, purple key: Nothing happens when you try to turn the key.

Door 3, red key: The key won't even turn.

Door 3, SHAW: That's not the right answer.

Door 3, SHOP: That successfully unlocks the door.

Door 3, SHOW: This attempt is not a triumphant one.

Door 3, SLAP: That's not correct.

Door 3, SLAW: The doorknob still won't turn.

Door 3, SLOP: This isn't it.

Door 3, STALWART: The lock stays locked.

Door 3, STRATEGO: Not the right answer.

Door 3, yellow key: Welp ... no.

Door 4, 3149: This isn't correct.

Door 4, 3337: A sad trombone noise plays to indicate "no."

Door 4, 4183: That attempt didn't work.

Door 4, 4757: This doesn't cause anything to happen.

Door 4, 5963: No, that's not it.

Door 4, 6319: You'll have to keep trying.

Door 4, CHIVE: Nope.

Door 4, CURVY: That wasn't it.

Door 4, GLASNOST: This is, unfortunately, wrong.

Door 4, GOALPOST: This doesn't do anything.

Door 4, HAIKU: Wish I had better news, but no.

Door 4, LIGHT: No luck.

Door 4, LYRIC: This doesn't do anything.

Door 4, MULCH: Not the answer.

Door 4, NORTHERN: That's not the answer.

Door 4, NOSTRILS: No luck this time.

Door 4, PORTUGAL: Not correct.

Door 4, POSTCARD: Try again.

Door 4, STALWART: This has no effect.

Door 4, STRATEGO: That wasn't the thing to do.

# List of National Parks

| | | |
|---|---|---|
| Acadia | Glacier | Mount Rainier |
| Arches | Grand Canyon | National Park of |
| Badlands | Grand Teton | American Samoa |
| Big Bend | Great Basin | New River Gorge |
| Biscayne | Great Sand Dunes | North Cascades |
| Black Canyon of the | Great Smoky | Olympic |
| Gunnison | Mountains | Petrified Forest |
| Bryce Canyon | Guadalupe Mountains | Pinnacles |
| Canyonlands | Haleakala | Redwood |
| Capitol Reef | Hawai'i Volcanoes | Rocky Mountain |
| Carlsbad Caverns | Hot Springs | Saguaro |
| Channel Islands | Indiana Dunes | Sequoia |
| Congaree | Isle Royale | Shenandoah |
| Crater Lake | Joshua Tree | Theodore Roosevelt |
| Cuyahoga Valley | Katmai | Virgin Islands |
| Death Valley | Kenai Fjords | Voyageurs |
| Denali | Kings Canyon | White Sands |
| Dry Tortugas | Kobuk Valley | Wind Cave |
| Everglades | Lake Clark | Wrangell-St. Elias |
| Gates of the Arctic | Lassen Volcanic | Yellowstone |
| Gateway Arch | Mammoth Cave | Yosemite |
| Glacier Bay | Mesa Verde | Zion |

# Morse Code Key

| | |
|---|---|
| A: •— | N: —• |
| B: —••• | O: ——— |
| C: —•—• | P: •——• |
| D: —•• | Q: ——•— |
| E: • | R: •—• |
| F: ••—• | S: ••• |
| G: ——• | T: — |
| H: •••• | U: ••— |
| I: •• | V: •••— |
| J: •——— | W: •—— |
| K: —•— | X: —••— |
| L: •—•• | Y: —•—— |
| M: —— | Z: ——•• |

# Hints

### 8 Ewan's "Distance Learning" hint

"Using numbers as indexes into a word is a common escape room trick—you know, like, say you had a list of movies that started with *Jaws 2* and *Spider-Man 3*. You'd try taking the second letter of "Jaws" and the third letter of "Spider-Man," giving you AI, which looks like it could be the beginning of something. I tried that on the signpost and the first few letters looked like gibberish, but then I thought, maybe the fact that it's a sign with arrows pointing in different directions is important."

### 14–15 "Shelf-Help Group" book list

The four books are *Gone Girl* by Gillian Flynn, *Marjorie Morningstar* by Herman Wouk, *Peter Pan* by J.M. Barrie, and *Silent Spring* by Rachel Carson.

### 18–19 Lily's "X Marks the Spot" instructions

"There are fifty 5-letter words in all caps in the Captain's Log, and these five grids can each fit ten words, five reading across and five reading down. I think we should try to fit them all in, and then hopefully we'll see what to do to find the password."

### 18–19 Malik's "X Marks the Spot" hint

"The chest says 'X Marks the Spot,' but there aren't any X's in any of these grids. Maybe we need to add the X's ourselves. Where could they go?"

### 20 Malik's "X Marks the Spot Again" hint

"I'm just saying, this time there *are* X's in the grid. Eight of them."

### 20 Olga's "X Marks the Spot Again" hint

"Well, we've tried looking at the digits in the solution and they aren't making anything useful—but they aren't the only numbers in the grid."

### 22–23 "Polly Gone" hint

Combining the answers to the Left and Right clues and finding a way to match them to the clues on the left will help identify the names that should go on the busts.

## 22–23 "Polly Gone" full instructions

Each bust on the left represents one of the busts on the shelf (plus one extra bust). The blanks indicate the length of the name on the bust. Combine the answers to the Left and Right clues; when correctly matched up, each pair will contain the answer to one of the clues inside the busts' heads; the unused letters on the outside of the pair will spell the name of the bust. For instance, if there was a bust of Charo with a clue inside reading "Domesticated animal related to the weasel," you could combine the Left answer CHAFER and the Right answer RETRO to make CHAFER+RETRO, which is FERRET inside CHARO.

## 22–23 "Polly Gone" final step hint

There are 14 musicians on the shelf and 15 busts. The last pair of Left and Right answers left over after all the rest are matched up should suggest another musician whose bust the group needs to find.

## 26 Juan's "Break It Up, Matey" recap

"One important thing is that the board must be a legal position, so there can't be pawns on the eighth rank, where they would promote and stop being pawns. That also means that Black can't already be in check, because Black just moved, and if Black had been in check, they would have had to get out of it somehow for the game to continue. And the white king can't be in check either, unless the checkmating move somehow gets White out of check."

## 26 Lily's "Break It Up, Matey" hint

"One common way to indicate squares on a chessboard is with coordinates—like, the lower left square is a1, and the upper right is h8. But these rows and columns are labeled completely differently."

## 27 Extra "Knight Game" givens

Add an 8 in the center square of the third row, and a 5 in the center square of the seventh row.

## 27 Kamala's "No Algebra" idea

"All the answers to these clues that I've come up with are five letters long, and they all start with abbreviations for chess pieces. Maybe we can match them up with the chess moves somehow."

## 29 Lily's "Words of Wisdom" hint

"All the capitalized names are hidden in the main part of Queenie's article, but they're hard to find, because each one has an extra letter stuck inside it. Those extra letters spell a message that must be a hint to the password, but I don't see what to do with it."

## 29 Nelson's "Words of Wisdom" password hint

"I think we need to interpret this literally. The first word sounds like it might be an instruction to remove something from the other words."

## 42 Olga's "Case of Emergency" explanation

"Well, first I noticed the lock has a picture of the Sun on it. And so I started thinking, well, there are eight planets, and we have eight phrases ..." (If that's enough of a hint for you, stop reading; otherwise continue on for full instructions.) "... so then I noticed that you can find the letters of all the planets in the phrases. In fact, every phrase can be anagrammed to spell a planet plus a number."

## 44 Ichiko's "Star Search" suggestion

"I can see bits and pieces of the words in the grid. If we add stars on top of some of the letters, with each star representing the letters S-T-A-R, then I bet we'll be able to find everything in the list."

## 44 Ewan's "Star Search" observation

"It looks like the letters we didn't circle spell something!"

## 45 Rosalie's "Constellation Prize" hints

"First, I'll tell you that the number of stars in each constellation corresponds to the number of different letters in one of the phrases. For instance, SPACE CAMP contains six different letters, and it corresponds to the constellation with six stars." (If that's enough information for you, stop reading; otherwise continue on for full instructions.) "Specifically, for each constellation, assign a single letter to every star so that, by following the paths from star to star, you can spell one of the six phrases."

## 52 Greg's "Tee Ceremony" hint

"Feel free to use an external reference. The room had an atlas in it, in case we needed it."

## 48–49 "Landing of the Lost" control panel (upside-down for fewer spoilers)

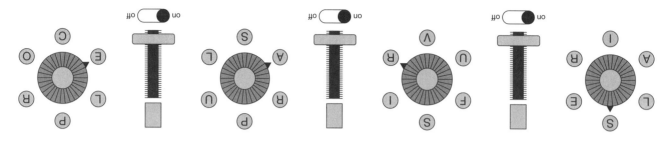

### 54 "Cheat Codes" starting hint

The lengths of the cheat codes are related to the lengths of the video games' names. It's also worth noting that the grid doesn't contain any A's or B's.

### 54 "Cheat Codes" instructions

All the video games are hidden in the grid, but they do not follow straight lines; they each follow a path that turns up, down, left, and right according to one of the cheat codes in the list. Additionally, the letters A and B do not appear in the grid; whenever an A or B appears in a video game's name, the cheat code indicates that letter instead of a direction.

### 54 "Cheat Codes" final step hint

Notice that each cheat code begins with a direction that brings you to the first letter of the video game. To follow that direction, you must have traveled from another letter. You might think of those letters as "start" letters.

### 55 Ciara's "Counter Intuitive" idea

"I've seen lots of puzzles where you try to spell 7-letter words with phone numbers, but I think this time we should try matching up the phone numbers with the initials to spell 9-letter words. Oh, you'd already figured that out? Well, maybe you'd rather hear my other idea."

### 55 Ciara's other "Counter Intuitive" idea

"There's something about these words that reminds me of some of the prizes behind the counter."

### 56–57 Ewan's "That's the Ticket" observation

"Why did the ticket redemption machine give us this receipt? It must be important that we have a copy of the order of the tickets."

# About the Authors

FRANCIS HEANEY is executive editor of Puzzlewright Press, a contributing writer and editor for the indie puzzle venue AVCX, and has been an editor-at-large for *Games* magazine and an ancillary writer for *Who Wants to Be a Millionaire?*. Their puzzles have appeared in *The New York Times*, *Entertainment Weekly*, *Wired*, *Time Out*, *The Wall Street Journal*, Al-Jazeera, and more; they have written over a dozen puzzle books. They live in New York City.

SCOTT WEISS is an assistant professor of computer science at Mount Saint Mary's University in Emmitsburg, Maryland. In his spare time, he and his son Em write and run audio escape rooms; find out more at www.squonkland.net. He's also responsible for the only non-zero three-way tie in *Jeopardy!* history. He lives with his family in Walkersville, Maryland.